MOUNJARO DIET COOKBOOK For BEGINNERS

250+ Easy and Delicious Recipes to Support Weight Loss, Manage Blood Sugar, and Boost Energy

© COPYRIGHT 2025 ALL RIGHT RESERVED
BY **Lila Reinger**

TABLE OF CONTENT

INTRODUCTION 6

Getting Started with the Mounjaro Diet 7
Traditional Kitchen Tools & Tricks 7

1. Cheesy Cauliflower Fritters 9
2. Creamy Garlic Spinach Chicken 9
3. Pesto Chicken Zoodle Bowls 9
4. Spinach and Cheese Frittata 10
5. Spicy Tuna Zoodle Bowls 10
6. Lemon Garlic Shrimp Skewers 10
7. Avocado Kale Salad 11
8. Bacon-Wrapped Asparagus 11
9. Creamy Tomato Zoodle Soup 11
10. Creamy Broccoli Cheddar Casserole ... 12
11. Creamy Mushroom Chicken Thighs 12
12. Lemon Pepper Chicken Drumsticks 13
13. Spaghetti Squash with Meat Sauce 13
14. Avocado Tuna Lettuce Wraps 13
15. Lemon Garlic Tilapia 14
16. Grilled Chicken Zoodle Bowl 14
17. Zucchini and Spinach Frittata 14
18. Creamy Pesto Cauliflower Bake 15
19. Lemon Herb Roasted Shrimp 15
20. Parmesan Crusted Tilapia 15
21. Parmesan Asparagus Fries 16
22. Garlic Roasted Cauliflower Mash 16
23. Keto Egg Muffins 16
24. Roasted Brussels Sprouts with Bacon . 17
25. Mediterranean Chopped Salad 17
26. Low-Carb Chicken Cordon Bleu 18
27. Cauliflower Mashed "Potatoes" 18
28. Sausage and Kale Soup 18
29. Cauliflower Gnocchi with Pesto 19
30. Cucumber and Avocado Gazpacho 19
31. Low-Carb Clam Chowder 19
32. Creamy Spinach Dip 20
33. Roasted Cabbage Wedges 20
34. Zesty Lemon Chicken Thighs 20
35. Garlic Parmesan Crusted Pork Chops . 20
36. Thai Peanut Zoodle Stir-Fry 21
37. Garlic Butter Chicken Thighs 21
38. Buffalo Cauliflower Tacos 22
39. Lemon Pepper Zucchini Chips 22
40. Roasted Eggplant Dip 22
41. Zoodle and Meatball Marinara 23
42. Grilled Shrimp Caesar Salad 23
43. Grilled Teriyaki Salmon 23
44. Avocado Tuna Salad 24
45. Lemon Dill Baked Cod 24
46. Cauliflower Pizza Bites 24
47. Zucchini and Turkey Skillet 25
48. Mediterranean Stuffed Bell Peppers .. 25
49. Low-Carb Shrimp Fajitas 26
50. Low-Carb Chicken Tikka Masala 26
51. Cauliflower Hummus 26
52. Creamy Roasted Red Pepper Soup 27
53. Garlic Herb Zucchini Chips 27
54. Spaghetti Squash Pad Thai 27
55. Grilled Steak with Cauliflower Mash .. 28
56. Roasted Cauliflower Steak 28
57. Slow-Cooker Lemon Herb Chicken 29
58. Garlic Roasted Brussels Sprouts 29
59. Garlic Butter Baked Salmon 29
60. Pesto Grilled Shrimp 29
61. Thai Coconut Shrimp Soup 30
62. Avocado Chocolate Smoothie 30
63. Turkey Taco Lettuce Cups 30
64. Dill Lemon Chicken Salad 31
65. Zoodle Alfredo with Chicken 31
66. Cabbage Slaw with Cilantro Dressing . 32
67. Roasted Garlic Cauliflower Soup 32
68. Low-Carb Meatball Zoodles 32
69. Tuscan Kale and Sausage Soup 33
70. Low-Carb Philly Cheesesteak Skillet ... 33
71. Creamy Broccoli Cauliflower Casserole 34
72. Baked Lemon Herb Salmon 34
73. Creamy Garlic Shrimp and Spinach 35
74. Roasted Veggie Buddha Bowl 35
75. Spicy Korean Cauliflower Wings 36
76. Lemon Butter Asparagus 36
77. Zucchini Grilled Cheese 37
78. Keto Cheeseburger Soup 37
79. Broccoli Cheddar Frittata 38
80. Salmon and Spinach Omelet 38
81. Pesto Stuffed Chicken Breasts 39
82. Roasted Garlic Parmesan Broccoli 39
83. Grilled Steak Salad with Avocado 40
84. Thai Peanut Zoodle Salad 40
85. Low-Carb Beef and Veggie Stir-Fry 40
86. Greek Yogurt Tzatziki Sauce 41
87. Shrimp Stir-Fry with Zoodles 41
88. Creamy Lemon Garlic Scallops 42
89. Blackened Salmon with Avocado Salsa 42
90. Lemon Herb Zoodle Salad 43
91. Low-Carb Beef and Broccoli 43
92. Grilled Lemon Asparagus 44
93. Grilled Lemon Chicken Kabobs 44
94. Shrimp Scampi with Zoodles 44
95. Bacon-wrapped Brussels Sprouts 45
96. Garlic Butter Shrimp and Veggies 45

#	Recipe	Page
97.	Sausage and Pepper Bake	46
98.	Turkey Sausage and Eggplant Skillet	46
99.	Grilled Portobello Mushroom Burgers	47
100.	Herb-Crusted Grilled Tuna	47
101.	Avocado Egg Salad Cups	47
102.	Low-Carb Mushroom Risotto	47
103.	Thai Coconut Chicken Soup	48
104.	Cabbage Stir-Fry with Ground Beef	48
105.	Grilled Chicken Caesar Salad	49
106.	Avocado Egg Breakfast Cups	49
107.	Lemon Garlic Chicken Stir-Fry	49
108.	Sesame Cauliflower Bites	49
109.	Low-Carb Eggplant Lasagna	50
110.	Caprese Stuffed Portobello Mushrooms	50
111.	Low-Carb Beef Stroganoff	50
112.	Buffalo Chicken Zucchini Boats	50
113.	Teriyaki Zoodle Bowls	51
114.	Creamy Cauliflower Mac and Cheese	51
115.	Beef and Mushroom Stir-Fry	51
116.	Zucchini Noodles with Lemon Garlic Shrimp	52
117.	Garlic Butter Roasted Mushrooms	52
118.	Turkey Sausage Breakfast Bowl	52
119.	Spinach Artichoke Dip	52
120.	Baked Garlic Parmesan Zucchini	53
121.	Low-Carb Cheeseburger Casserole	53
122.	Pesto Cauliflower Mash	53
123.	Creamy Coconut Curry Shrimp	53
124.	Keto Chocolate Avocado Mousse	54
125.	Cauliflower Gratin	54
126.	Spinach Artichoke Chicken Casserole	54
127.	Low-Carb Shrimp Pad Thai	55
128.	Creamy Cauliflower Soup	55
129.	Garlic Butter Broccoli Casserole	55
130.	Grilled Chicken and Veggie Skewers	55
131.	Shrimp Avocado Lettuce Wraps	56
132.	Garlic Butter Mushrooms and Spinach	56
133.	Cauliflower Crust Margherita Pizza	56
134.	Cajun Grilled Shrimp Skewers	57
135.	Cauliflower Hash Browns	57
136.	Zoodle Caprese Salad	57
137.	Lemon Butter Cod with Spinach	57
138.	Creamy Spinach and Mushroom Soup	58
139.	Teriyaki Chicken Stir-Fry	58
140.	Eggplant Parmesan Stacks	58
141.	Grilled Lemon Herb Chicken Breasts	59
142.	Buffalo Cauliflower Wings	59
143.	Roasted Radish and Zucchini	60
144.	Spinach and Avocado Smoothie	60
145.	Baked Herb-Crusted Salmon	60
146.	Sesame Ginger Cucumber Salad	60
147.	Mediterranean Egg Muffins	61
148.	Grilled Salmon Caesar Salad	61
149.	Avocado Bacon Salad	61
150.	Grilled Lemon Shrimp Salad	62
151.	Grilled Steak and Veggie Skewers	62
152.	Lemon Dill Roasted Chicken	63
153.	Avocado Lime Chicken Salad	63
154.	Keto Zoodle Stir-Fry	63
155.	Baked Feta and Spinach Casserole	64
156.	Shrimp and Avocado Salad	64
157.	Cheesy Cauliflower Casserole	64
158.	Lemon Herb Crusted Salmon	65
159.	Avocado Deviled Eggs	65
160.	Garlic Parmesan Kale Chips	66
161.	Lemon Thyme Roasted Veggies	66
162.	Low-Carb Shepherd's Pie	66
163.	Low-Carb Baked Ziti	67
164.	Zoodle Veggie Stir-Fry	67
165.	Low-Carb Crab Cakes	67
166.	Keto Spinach Artichoke Dip	68
167.	Roasted Garlic and Herb Cauliflower	68
168.	Low-Carb Tortilla Soup	68
169.	Almond-Crusted Baked Chicken	69
170.	Zoodle Primavera	69
171.	Spinach and Feta Stuffed Peppers	70
172.	Parmesan Crusted Chicken Tenders	70
173.	Broccoli Cheddar Soup	70
174.	Lemon Garlic Butter Scallops	71
175.	Spaghetti Squash Zoodle Combo	71
176.	Cheesy Zucchini Boats	72
177.	Bacon-Wrapped Pork Tenderloin	72
178.	Low-Carb Chicken Taco Skillet	72
179.	Baked Herb Chicken Wings	73
180.	Creamy Lemon Zoodle Alfredo	73
181.	Lemon Thyme Grilled Chicken	73
182.	Keto Cauliflower Fried Rice	74
183.	Zucchini Lasagna Rolls	74
184.	Asian Chicken Cabbage Stir-Fry	74
185.	Creamy Tomato Basil Soup	75
186.	Roasted Garlic Zoodle Salad	75
187.	Jalapeño Popper Stuffed Mushrooms	76
188.	Zoodle Stir-Fry with Pork	76
189.	Eggplant Zoodle Parmesan	76
190.	Greek Turkey Meatball Bowls	77
191.	Thai Zoodle Chicken Soup	77
192.	Grilled Tuna Steak with Herb Butter	78
193.	Cauliflower Rice Risotto	78
194.	Keto Chocolate Chia Pudding	78
195.	Garlic Parmesan Chicken Wings	79
196.	Zoodle Chicken Stir-Fry	79
197.	Low-Carb Chicken Alfredo Bake	79
198.	Cauliflower Crust Breakfast Pizza	80
199.	Asian Cucumber Salad	80
200.	Keto Stuffed Bell Peppers	80
201.	Low-Carb Cabbage Stir-Fry	81
202.	Creamy Spinach Stuffed Mushrooms	81
203.	Asian Sesame Chicken Lettuce Wraps	81
204.	Spaghetti Squash Puttanesca	82
205.	Baked Parmesan Eggplant Slices	82
206.	Caprese Salad with Balsamic Glaze	83

#	Title	Page
207.	Low-Carb French Onion Soup	83
208.	Creamy Spinach Artichoke Dip	83
209.	Roasted Cauliflower Tabbouleh	84
210.	Spaghetti Squash with Pesto	84
211.	Creamy Garlic Herb Dip	84
212.	Herb-crusted whitefish	85
213.	Roasted Veggie and Shrimp Skillet	85
214.	Lemon Thyme Grilled Vegetables	85
215.	Avocado Bacon Chicken Salad	86
216.	Cauliflower Pizza with Pesto	86
217.	Mediterranean Zoodle Salad	86
218.	Pesto Zoodle Bowl	87
219.	Broccoli Slaw Stir-Fry	87
220.	Zoodle Stir-Fry with Tofu	88
221.	Cheesy Zucchini Casserole	88
222.	Cauliflower "Risotto" with Mushrooms	88
223.	Greek Chicken Gyro Bowls	89
224.	Creamy Tuscan Salmon	89
225.	Cucumber Dill Yogurt Salad	89
226.	Chicken Zoodle Pho	90
227.	Cucumber Mint Yogurt Salad	90
228.	Chicken and Broccoli Alfredo Bake	90
229.	Herb-Crusted Pork Chops	91
230.	Herb-Crusted Grilled Salmon	91
231.	Spaghetti Squash Carbonara	91
232.	Chili Lime Grilled Shrimp	92
233.	Cilantro Lime Cauliflower Rice	92
234.	Turkey Zucchini Meatballs	92
235.	Cheesy Spinach and Egg Bake	93
236.	Avocado Egg Salad Lettuce Wraps	93
237.	Keto Zucchini Bread	93
238.	Garlic Lemon Broiled Shrimp	94
239.	Pesto Shrimp Salad	94
240.	Herb Butter Roasted Turkey	94
241.	Roasted Cauliflower Curry	95
242.	Grilled Halloumi Salad	95
243.	Low-Carb Stuffed Cabbage Rolls	95
244.	Crispy Baked Tofu Nuggets	96
245.	Herb Butter Baked Trout	96
246.	Asian Grilled Chicken Skewers	96
247.	Shrimp Zoodle Scampi	97
248.	Sesame Chicken Cauliflower Rice	97

THE END 98

INTRODUCTION

A must-have resource for anybody looking to reduce weight and keep healthy is the Mounjaro Diet Cookbook for Beginners. It will show you how to make meals that are tasty, filling, and full of nutrients. Whether you're new to Mounjaro (tripeptide) or just want some new meals to eat while you're on the pill, this cookbook has everything you need to get the most out of this potent medicine. The recipes are simple to follow & will keep you full, energetic, and on schedule.

People with type 2 diabetes, in particular, may benefit from the weight management and blood sugar control features offered by the FDA-approved medicine Mounjaro. It helps with hunger suppression, metabolic enhancement, and long-term weight reduction by imitating the body's natural hormones that control insulin and food intake. Nevertheless, a healthy lifestyle and a well-balanced diet should be supplemented with Mounjaro for optimal outcomes. Here's a cookbook that can help with that!

Lean meats, fiber-rich veggies, healthy fats, minimally processed foods, and added sugars are the hallmarks of this beginner-friendly cookbook. These meals are designed to keep you going strong, keep temptations at bay, and meet all of your nutritional requirements while climbing Mount Everest. Find alternatives that fit well with your new lifestyle, whether you're desiring a robust breakfast, a fulfilling lunch, or a gourmet supper.

A delicious, nutritious food that doesn't need a lot of special equipment or materials is here. Whether you're feeding a family or just yourself, these recipes will make it easier to establish and maintain good eating habits.

How about we go on this adventure side by side? If you follow the advice in this cookbook and make healthy eating choices, you can lose weight & improve your health without sacrificing taste.

GETTING STARTED WITH THE MOUNJARO DIET

The Mounjaro Diet is designed to support those using Mounjaro (Tirzepatide) for weight management and blood sugar control. It focuses on nutrient-dense, balanced meals that help maintain energy levels, support metabolic health, and promote sustainable weight loss.

❖ **Key Principles of the Mounjaro Diet:**

- **Prioritize Lean Proteins** – For fullness and muscle preservation, try eating protein-rich foods like chicken, turkey, fish, eggs, and plants.

- **Focus on Fiber-Rich Foods** – A diet rich in beans, vegetables, and whole grains aids digestion and glucose regulation.

- **Healthy Fats are Essential** – Good fats for your heart may be found in avocados, almonds, seeds, and olive oil.

- **Limit Processed Carbs and Sugars** – Blood sugar spikes and crashes may be avoided by reducing processed carbohydrates.

- **Hydration is Key** – Dehydration is prevalent with Mounjaro usage; drinking plenty of water helps digestion and avoids it.

- **Meal Timing Matters** – Maintaining energy and reducing cravings are both helped by eating balanced meals at regular intervals.

TRADITIONAL KITCHEN TOOLS & TRICKS

You don't need fancy gadgets to follow the Mounjaro Diet. Simple kitchen tools and smart cooking techniques make meal prep easier and more enjoyable.

❖ Essential Kitchen Tools:

- Cast Iron Skillet – An ideal choice for preparing one-pan dishes and searing meats.

- Dutch Oven – Ideal for sauces, stews, and dishes cooked slowly.

- Food Scale – Aids in controlling food intake to avoid obesity.

- Sharp Chef's Knife – Essential for quick and easy protein and vegetable cutting.

- Blender or Immersion Blender – Works well in sauces, soups, and smoothies.

- Mason Jars or Meal Prep Containers – These are places to keep prepared foods and any leftovers.

❖ Cooking Tricks for Success:

- **Batch Cooking:** Make a big pot of protein, grain, and vegetable stock to have on hand for weeknight dinners.

- **Sheet Pan Meals:** Make supper in a flash by roasting your steak and vegetables at the same time.

- **Use Low-Sodium Broths:** Adds taste without adding too much salt.

- **Spice It Up:** Without increasing calorie or carb intake, herbs and spices enhance flavor.

- **Steam & Roast Instead of Frying:** It ensures that food is nutritious and full of healthy ingredients.

- **Portion Before Eating:** Assists in practicing mindful eating and curbs excessive food intake.

1. CHEESY CAULIFLOWER FRITTERS

Total Time: 30 minutes | Prep Time: 10 minutes

Ingredients:

- 2 cups riced cauliflower
- ¼ cup grated Parmesan cheese
- ¼ cup almond flour
- ½ teaspoon salt
- 2 tablespoons olive oil
- ½ cup shredded cheddar cheese
- 2 eggs
- 1 teaspoon garlic powder
- ½ teaspoon black pepper

Directions:

(1) Combine the riced cauliflower, pepper, eggs, almond flour, cheddar, Parmesan, garlic powder, and salt in a bowl. **(2)** While the pan is on middle heat, add the olive oil and cook it through. **(3)** Shape a spoonful of the mixture into a fritter in the pan by pressing it down. **(4)** After 3–4 minutes on each side, the food should be crispy and golden brown. **(5)** Remove from pan & set aside to drain on paper towel. Warm sour cream or Greek yogurt makes a great accompaniment.

2. CREAMY GARLIC SPINACH CHICKEN

Total Time: 35 minutes | Prep Time: 10 minutes

Ingredients:

- 2 boneless, skinless chicken breasts
- 3 cloves garlic, minced
- ½ cup heavy cream
- ½ teaspoon salt
- 1 tablespoon olive oil
- 1 cup fresh spinach, chopped
- ¼ cup grated Parmesan cheese
- ½ teaspoon black pepper
- ½ teaspoon red pepper flakes (optional)

Directions:

(1) Oil a skillet & set it over medium heat. **(2)** Add salt & pepper to the chicken breasts and sear them for 5 to 6 minutes on each side or until they get a golden brown color. Detach and put aside. **(3)** Put the garlic in the same pan and cook it for a minute. **(4)** After around two minutes, add the spinach and simmer until it wilts. **(5)** Mix in the Parmesan cheese after adding the heavy cream. Simmer for two to three minutes. **(6)** Put the chicken back in the pan and cook it for another 5 minutes at a simmer. **(7)** Accompany with heated cauliflower rice or roasted veggies for a side dish.

3. PESTO CHICKEN ZOODLE BOWLS

Total Time: 25 minutes | Prep Time: 10 minutes

Ingredients:

- 2 boneless, skinless chicken breasts, sliced
- 2 tablespoons olive oil
- ¼ cup cherry tomatoes, halved
- ¼ teaspoon black pepper
- 2 medium zucchini, spiralized
- ¼ cup basil pesto
- ¼ teaspoon salt
- 2 tablespoons grated Parmesan cheese

Directions:

(1) One tablespoon of olive oil may be warmed in a pan and placed over medium heat. Prepare the chicken for another 5 to 6 minutes or until done, adding salt and pepper as needed. Take it out of the oven. **(2)** Sauté the zucchini noodles for 2 minutes, turning regularly, in the same pan with the remaining olive oil. Toss the cooked chicken with the pesto sauce and return it to the pan. **(3)** Cook for a further minute after stirring in cherry tomatoes. **(4)** Take it off the stove, top it with Parmesan, and serve it hot.

4. SPINACH AND CHEESE FRITTATA

Total Time: 30 minutes | Prep Time: 10 minutes

Ingredients:

6 eggs	½ cup milk (or unsweetened almond milk)
1 cup fresh spinach, chopped	½ cup shredded mozzarella cheese
¼ cup grated Parmesan cheese	½ teaspoon salt
¼ teaspoon black pepper	1 tablespoon olive oil

Directions:

(1) Get your oven preheated to 375°F, which is 190°C. **(2)** Beat the eggs, milk, pepper, and salt together in a bowl. **(3)** With an oven-safe skillet set over medium heat, warm the olive oil. **(4)** After around two minutes, add the spinach and simmer until it wilts. **(5)** Once the spinach is coated with the egg mixture, heat for two or three minutes or until the edges begin to firm. **(6)** Distribute the Parmesan and mozzarella cheeses equally over the surface. **(7)** After 15 to 18 minutes, the frittata should be completely set. Place the pan in the oven. **(8)** Take it out of the oven, give it a minute to cool, and then cut it into wedges. Keep heated before serving.

5. SPICY TUNA ZOODLE BOWLS

Total Time: 20 minutes | Prep Time: 10 minutes | Cook Time: 10 minutes

Ingredients:

2 cans of tuna in water, drained	2 medium zucchini, spiralized
1 tablespoon olive oil	1 teaspoon sesame oil
1 tablespoon sriracha	2 tablespoons low-sodium soy sauce
1 teaspoon grated ginger	1 teaspoon minced garlic
1/2 teaspoon red pepper flakes	1/4 cup shredded carrots
1/4 cup chopped scallions	1/2 avocado, sliced
1 teaspoon sesame seeds (for garnish)	

Directions:

(1) To get the best results, warm the olive oil in a skillet over medium heat. Toss in the spiralized zucchini and cook for two or three minutes or until just barely softened. **(2)** Take it out of the oven. **(3)** The drained tuna, sriracha, soy sauce, sesame oil, ginger, garlic, and red pepper flakes should all be combined in a bowl. Mix thoroughly. **(4)** Before topping each dish with zoodles, spoon the spicy tuna mixture over. **(5)** Incorporate scallions, shredded carrots, avocado pieces, and sesame seeds as garnishes. Make sure to serve right away.

6. LEMON GARLIC SHRIMP SKEWERS

Total Time: 15 minutes | Prep Time: 10 minutes | Cook Time: 5 minutes

Ingredients:

1 lb large shrimp, peeled and deveined	2 tablespoons olive oil
2 tablespoons fresh lemon juice	2 cloves garlic, minced
1 teaspoon smoked paprika	1/2 teaspoon salt

1/4 teaspoon black pepper	1/4 teaspoon red pepper flakes (optional)
2 tablespoons chopped fresh parsley	Lemon wedges for serving
Skewers: if using wooden skewers	

Directions:

(1) Toss the olive oil, garlic, lemon juice, paprika, salt, black pepper, & red pepper flakes in a bowl and stir to combine. *(2)* Coat the shrimp by tossing them in the marinade. Set aside for five minutes. *(3)* First, get a grill or grill pan hot over medium-high heat. Then, thread the shrimp onto sticks. *(4)* To make the shrimp opaque and pink, grill the skewers for two to three minutes on each side. *(5)* After removing from the heat, garnish with chopped parsley. Cut into wedges and serve.

7. AVOCADO KALE SALAD

Total Time: 10 minutes | Prep Time: 10 minutes

Ingredients:

4 cups kale, chopped	1 ripe avocado, diced
1/4 cup cherry tomatoes, halved	1/4 cup cucumber, diced
1/4 cup red onion, thinly sliced	2 tablespoons feta cheese (optional)
1 tablespoon sunflower seeds or pumpkin seeds	1 tablespoon extra virgin olive oil
1 tablespoon lemon juice	1/2 teaspoon Dijon mustard
1/4 teaspoon salt	1/4 teaspoon black pepper

Directions:

(1) Chop the kale and place it in a big basin. Toss the greens with half a spoonful of olive oil and give it a good massage for a minute or two to soften. *(2)* Combine with cucumber, feta cheese (if desired), avocado, cherry tomatoes, and sunflower seeds. *(3)* Combine the lemon juice, Dijon mustard, salt, black pepper, & the remaining olive oil in a small bowl and whisk to combine. *(4)* Toss the salad to blend after adding the dressing. Serve right away.

8. BACON-WRAPPED ASPARAGUS

Total Time: 20 minutes | Prep Time: 5 minutes | Cook Time: 15 minutes

Ingredients:

1 bunch asparagus (about 12 spears), trimmed	6 slices bacon, cut in half
1/2 teaspoon garlic powder	1/4 teaspoon black pepper
1/2 teaspoon smoked paprika	1 teaspoon olive oil

Directions:

(1) Set oven temperature to 400°F. Sprinkle parchment paper on a baking pan. *(2)* Wrap half a piece of bacon around each spear of asparagus, being sure to secure the ends beneath. *(3)* Place the asparagus bundles on the baking pan. Add a little olive oil & season with smoky paprika, black pepper, and garlic powder. *(4)* The bacon should be crispy, and the asparagus should be tender, so bake them for 12 to 15 minutes. *(5)* As an appetizer or side dish, serve warm.

9. CREAMY TOMATO ZOODLE SOUP

Total Time: 25 minutes | Prep Time: 10 minutes

Ingredients:

2 medium zucchini, spiralized	1 can (14.5 oz) diced tomatoes

1 cup unsweetened almond milk	1 cup low-sodium vegetable broth
2 cloves garlic, minced	1/2 small onion, chopped
1 tbsp olive oil	1/2 tsp dried basil
1/2 tsp dried oregano	1/2 tsp sea salt
1/4 tsp black pepper	1/4 tsp red pepper flakes (optional)
1/4 cup heavy cream	

Directions:

(1) Put the olive oil in a pot and place it over medium heat. Saute the garlic & onions until they are tender. *(2)* Toss in some salt, pepper, basil, oregano, vegetable broth, sliced tomatoes, and veggies. Cook, covered, at a low simmer for 10 minutes. *(3)* Before blending with an immersion blender, whisk in the heavy cream and almond milk. *(4)* Cook the spiralized zucchini (zoodles) for three to four minutes or until they are soft. *(5)* Season to taste and serve warm.

10. CREAMY BROCCOLI CHEDDAR CASSEROLE

Total Time: 40 minutes | Prep Time: 10 minutes

Ingredients:

4 cups broccoli florets	1 cup shredded sharp cheddar cheese
1/2 cup heavy cream	1/2 cup unsweetened almond milk
2 tbsp cream cheese	2 cloves garlic, minced
1/4 cup grated Parmesan cheese	1 tbsp olive oil
1/2 tsp sea salt	1/4 tsp black pepper
1/4 tsp ground mustard	1/2 tsp smoked paprika

Directions:

(1) Get your oven preheated to 375°F, which is 190°C. Apply olive oil to a baking dish. *(2)* After 5 minutes of steaming, the broccoli should be just soft enough to transfer to the baking dish. *(3)* Melt the olive oil in a skillet set over medium heat. Toss in the garlic and sauté until it begins to smell good. *(4)* Whisk in the almond milk, heavy cream, and cream cheese until combined. *(5)* Season with salt, pepper, mustard, paprika, Parmesan, and cheddar. Mash the cheese until it melts. *(6)* Toss the broccoli with the cheese sauce so it coats evenly. *(7)* Cook in the oven for 20 minutes or until the top is brown and the inside is bubbling. Keep heated before serving.

11. CREAMY MUSHROOM CHICKEN THIGHS

Total Time: 35 minutes | Prep Time: 10 minutes

Ingredients:

4 bone-in, skin-on chicken thighs	1 cup mushrooms, sliced
1/2 cup heavy cream	1/2 cup chicken broth, low sodium
2 tbsp olive oil	2 tbsp butter
2 cloves garlic, minced	1/2 small onion, chopped
1 tsp dried thyme	1/2 tsp salt
1/4 tsp black pepper	1/4 tsp red pepper flakes (optional)

Directions:

(1) Toss the olive oil into a large pan and heat it over medium-high heat. Add salt and pepper to the chicken. *(2)* Flip the chicken thighs over and sear them for another 5 minutes on each side or until they become golden brown. Detach and put aside. *(3)* While the butter is melting, sauté the garlic, mushrooms, and onions in the same pan until they are tender. *(4)* Toss in the chicken stock, thyme, and red pepper flakes. Low heat for five minutes. *(5)* After you've mixed in the heavy cream, put the chicken back in the pan. *(6)* Reduce heat and simmer for ten to 15 minutes, or until chicken

is done and sauce thickens. *(7)* Warm it up and serve it with some steamed greens or cauliflower rice on the side.

12. LEMON PEPPER CHICKEN DRUMSTICKS

Total Time: 45 minutes | Prep Time: 10 minutes

Ingredients:

6 chicken drumsticks	2 tbsp olive oil
2 tbsp lemon juice	1 tbsp lemon zest
1 tsp garlic powder	1 tsp onion powder
1 tsp lemon pepper seasoning	1/2 tsp sea salt
1/2 tsp smoked paprika	1/4 tsp black pepper

Directions:

(1) Get your oven ready for 400°F or 200°C. Put parchment paper on a baking pan. *(2)* Combine extra-virgin olive oil, zest, juice, garlic powder, onion powder, lemon pepper, salt, paprika, and black pepper in a casserole dish. *(3)* Coat the drumsticks well with the marinade by tossing them in it. *(4)* Bake the drumsticks for 35 to 40 minutes, turning them over halfway through or until they are crispy and fully cooked. *(5)* Warm it up and top it with some roasted veggies or a side salad.

13. SPAGHETTI SQUASH WITH MEAT SAUCE

Total Time: 50 minutes | Prep Time: 10 minutes

Ingredients:

1 medium spaghetti squash	1 lb lean ground turkey or beef
1 small onion, diced	2 cloves garlic, minced
1 can (14.5 oz) diced tomatoes	1/2 cup tomato sauce
1/2 tsp dried oregano	1/2 tsp dried basil
1/2 tsp salt	1/4 tsp black pepper
1 tbsp olive oil	1/4 cup grated Parmesan cheese

Directions:

(1) Set oven temperature to 400°F. After removing the seeds, cut the spaghetti squash lengthwise in half. Before placing the cut side down on a baking pan, brush with olive oil. Poach for 35 to 40 minutes or until soft. *(2)* Get a pan going over medium heat while you roast the squash. Brown the ground meat (turkey or beef) and crumble it into the mixture. *(3)* While the garlic and onion are softening, add them to the skillet. Season with salt & pepper, then stir in tomato sauce, oregano, basil, chopped tomatoes, and salt. Let it simmer for ten minutes. *(4)* After the spaghetti squash has cooked through, remove its threads using a fork. Place in individual dishes and drizzle with beef sauce. If you want, you may top it with Parmesan.

14. AVOCADO TUNA LETTUCE WRAPS

Total Time: 10 minutes | Prep Time: 10 minutes

Ingredients:

1 can (5 oz) tuna in water, drained	1/2 ripe avocado, mashed
1 tbsp Greek yogurt or mayonnaise	1 tsp Dijon mustard
1/2 tsp lemon juice	1/4 tsp garlic powder
1/4 tsp salt	1/8 tsp black pepper
4 large romaine or butter lettuce leaves	1/4 cup diced cucumber
1/4 cup diced tomatoes	

Directions:

(1) Gather all the ingredients in a dish and combine them: mashed avocado, Greek yogurt (or mayonnaise), lemon juice, Dijon mustard, garlic powder, salt, and pepper. *(2)* After you've spread out the lettuce, top with the tuna mixture. *(3)* Sprinkle chopped tomatoes and cucumber on top. *(4)* Prepare and serve the wraps right away by rolling them up or folding them like tacos.

15. LEMON GARLIC TILAPIA

Total Time: 20 minutes | Prep Time: 5 minutes

Ingredients:

2 tilapia fillets	1 tbsp olive oil
1 tbsp fresh lemon juice	2 cloves garlic, minced
1/2 tsp paprika	1/4 tsp salt
1/4 tsp black pepper	1/2 tsp dried parsley (or fresh)
Lemon wedges for serving	

Directions:

(1) Get your oven preheated to 375°F, which is 190°C. Sprinkle parchment paper on a baking pan. *(2)* Arrange the fillets of tilapia on the baking pan. Toss with the lemon juice & olive oil. *(3)* After seasoning the fillets with salt, pepper, parsley, and chopped garlic, sprinkle with paprika. *(4)* The fish should be opaque and readily flaked with a fork after 12–15 minutes in the oven. *(5)* Garnish with lemon slices and serve hot.

16. GRILLED CHICKEN ZOODLE BOWL

Total Time: 25 minutes | Prep Time: 10 minutes

Ingredients:

2 boneless, skinless chicken breasts	1 tbsp olive oil
1/2 tsp garlic powder	1/2 tsp Italian seasoning
1/2 tsp salt	1/4 tsp black pepper
2 medium zucchini, spiralized	1/2 cup cherry tomatoes, halved
1/4 cup grated Parmesan cheese	1 tbsp balsamic vinegar

Directions:

(1) Preheat a pan or grill until it begins to sizzle. While the chicken breasts are marinating in olive oil, season them with salt, pepper, garlic powder, and Italian seasoning. *(2)* Once the chicken is done, cook it for another 6 to 7 minutes each side. Before slicing, remove it and let it rest for 5 minutes. *(3)* Cherry tomatoes, Parmesan cheese, balsamic vinegar, and spiralized zucchini (zoodles) should be mixed in a big basin. *(4)* Before serving, garnish with grilled chicken slices.

17. ZUCCHINI AND SPINACH FRITTATA

Total Time: 30 minutes | Prep Time: 10 minutes

Ingredients:

6 large eggs	½ cup unsweetened almond milk
1 medium zucchini, grated	1 cup fresh spinach, chopped
¼ cup feta cheese, crumbled	½ teaspoon garlic powder
½ teaspoon onion powder	½ teaspoon salt
¼ teaspoon black pepper	1 tablespoon olive oil

Directions:

(1) Get your oven preheated to 375°F, which is 190°C. *(2)* Coat the eggs and almond milk with a whisk in a bowl. Combine with salt, pepper,

onion, and garlic powders. *(3)* With an oven-safe skillet set over medium heat, warm the olive oil. Cook for another two or three minutes or until the spinach and grated zucchini are tender. *(4)* Top the veggies with the egg mixture. Top with some crumbled feta. *(5)* Allow to cook for two or three minutes in a skillet until the edges begin to harden. *(6)* After 15 to 18 minutes, or until the middle is firm, place the pan in the oven. *(7)* After letting it cool for a while, slice it. Keep heated before serving.

18. CREAMY PESTO CAULIFLOWER BAKE

Total Time: 35 minutes | Prep Time: 10 minutes

Ingredients:

1 medium head of cauliflower	½ cup Greek yogurt
¼ cup basil pesto	¼ cup grated Parmesan cheese
½ teaspoon garlic powder	½ teaspoon salt
¼ teaspoon black pepper	½ teaspoon red pepper flakes (optional)
1 tablespoon olive oil	

Directions:

(1) Achieve an oven temperature of 400°F. Drizzle some olive oil into a baking bowl. Cook the cauliflower florets for 5 minutes in a steamer or saucepan until they are just soft. Drainage hole *(2)* Combine the pesto, Greek yogurt, garlic powder, salt, and pepper in a bowl. *(3)* Distribute the pesto mixture evenly over the cauliflower and toss to coat. *(4)* After preparing the baking dish, transfer the mixture to it and top it with Parmesan cheese. *(5)* Once the top is brown and the bubbly begins to bubble, bake for another 20 to 25 minutes. *(6)* Allow it to cool for a short while before consumption.

19. LEMON HERB ROASTED SHRIMP

Total Time: 15 minutes | Prep Time: 5 minutes

Ingredients:

1 lb large shrimp, peeled and deveined	2 tablespoons olive oil
2 tablespoons fresh lemon juice	1 teaspoon lemon zest
2 cloves garlic, minced	½ teaspoon salt
¼ teaspoon black pepper	½ teaspoon dried oregano
½ teaspoon paprika	1 tablespoon fresh parsley, chopped

Directions:

(1) Set the oven temperature to 425°F. Sprinkle parchment paper on a baking pan. *(2)* A bowl should be used to whisk together the garlic, olive oil, lemon zest, lemon juice, salt, pepper, oregano, and paprika. After 5 minutes, toss the shrimp with the marinade. *(3)* Spread the shrimp out evenly on the baking pan. *(4)* To get a pink and fully cooked inside, roast for 8 to 10 minutes. *(5)* Serve right away with a sprinkle of fresh parsley.

20. PARMESAN CRUSTED TILAPIA

Total Time: 20 minutes | Prep Time: 5 minutes

Ingredients:

2 tilapia fillets	¼ cup grated Parmesan cheese
¼ cup almond flour	½ teaspoon garlic powder
½ teaspoon onion powder	½ teaspoon dried parsley
½ teaspoon salt	¼ teaspoon black

1 tablespoon olive oil | pepper
Lemon wedges for serving

Directions:

(1) Set oven temperature to 400°F. Sprinkle parchment paper on a baking pan. **(2)** Combine almond flour, Parmesan cheese, minced garlic and onions, dried parsley, salt, and pepper in a bowl. **(3)** Apply the Parmesan mixture evenly over the drained tilapia fillets. **(4)** Oil a skillet & set it over medium heat. Brown the fillets in a skillet over medium heat, 2 minutes on each side. **(5)** Bake the fillets for eight to 10 minutes or until they become flaky. **(6)** Cut into wedges and serve.

21. PARMESAN ASPARAGUS FRIES

Total Time: 25 minutes | Prep Time: 10 minutes

Ingredients:

1 bunch asparagus, trimmed	1/2 cup grated Parmesan cheese
1/2 cup almond flour	1/2 teaspoon garlic powder
1/2 teaspoon paprika	1/4 teaspoon salt
1/4 teaspoon black pepper	1 egg, beaten

Directions:

(1) Set oven temperature to 400°F. Sprinkle parchment paper on a baking pan. **(2)** Combine almond flour, Parmesan, garlic powder, paprika, salt, and pepper in a bowl. **(3)** Coat the asparagus spears with the Parmesan mixture after dipping them in the beaten egg. **(4)** Arrange the coated asparagus on the baking sheet that has been ready. **(5)** Toast until crisp and golden, about 15 minutes. **(6)** Warm it up and savor it!

22. GARLIC ROASTED CAULIFLOWER MASH

Total Time: 30 minutes | Prep Time: 10 minutes

Ingredients:

1 medium head cauliflower, cut into florets	3 cloves garlic, minced
2 tablespoons olive oil	1/4 cup heavy cream
1/4 cup grated Parmesan cheese	1/2 teaspoon salt
1/4 teaspoon black pepper	1 tablespoon unsalted butter

Directions:

(1) Get your oven preheated to 375°F, which is 190°C. Toss the cauliflower florets in a baking dish with the olive oil and garlic. **(2)** To get the soft meat, roast it for 20 minutes. **(3)** Fill a food processor with the roasted cauliflower. Include butter, salt, pepper, Parmesan, and heavy cream. **(4)** Whisk or mix until combined. **(5)** This low-carb mash substitute is wonderful when served warm.

23. KETO EGG MUFFINS

Total Time: 25 minutes | Prep Time: 10 minutes

Ingredients:

6 large eggs	1/4 cup heavy cream
1/2 cup shredded cheddar cheese	1/4 cup diced bell peppers
1/4 cup chopped spinach	1/4 teaspoon salt
1/4 teaspoon black pepper	1/2 teaspoon garlic powder

Directions:

(1) Get your oven preheated to 375°F, which is 190°C. Coat a muffin pan with oil. **(2)** Mash the eggs with the heavy cream, season with salt &

pepper, and add the garlic powder. *(3)* Combine spinach, bell peppers, and cheddar cheese. *(4)* Fill up each muffin pan cup three-quarters of the way to the top with batter. *(5)* The eggs should be set in the oven after 15 minutes. *(6)* Allow it to cool for a moment before you eat.

24. ROASTED BRUSSELS SPROUTS WITH BACON

Total Time: 30 minutes | Prep Time: 10 minutes

Ingredients:

1 lb Brussels sprouts, trimmed and halved	4 slices bacon, chopped
2 tablespoons olive oil	1/2 teaspoon salt
1/4 teaspoon black pepper	1/2 teaspoon garlic powder

Directions:

(1) Set oven temperature to 400°F. *(2)* Add garlic powder, salt, pepper, & olive oil to the Brussels sprouts. Toss to coat. Place on a baking pan. *(3)* Top the Brussels sprouts with chopped bacon. *(4)* Caramelize and crisp up in 20 minutes of roasting, tossing halfway through. *(5)* Quickly prepare and enjoy!

Recipe 5: Herb-Crusted Pork Tenderloin

Total Time: 35 minutes | Prep Time: 10 minutes

Ingredients:

1 pork tenderloin (about 1 lb)	2 tablespoons olive oil
1 tablespoon Dijon mustard	1 teaspoon dried rosemary
1 teaspoon dried thyme	1 teaspoon garlic powder
1/2 teaspoon salt	1/4 teaspoon black pepper

Directions:

(1) Set oven temperature to 400°F. *(2)* Before adding the thyme, rosemary, garlic powder, and garlic, season with salt and pepper. Dijon mustard should be rubbed into pork tenderloin before coating it with the herb mixture. *(3)* In a skillet that can be used in an oven, warm the olive oil over medium-high heat. Fry the pork for two minutes each side in a skillet over high heat. *(4)* Preheat oven to 145°F (63°C) and bake skillet for 20-25 minutes, or until done. *(5)* After 5 minutes, let aside to cool before cutting. Keep heated before serving.

25. MEDITERRANEAN CHOPPED SALAD

Total Time: 15 minutes | Prep Time: 15 minutes

Ingredients:

1 cup cherry tomatoes, halved	1 cucumber, diced
½ red onion, finely chopped	½ cup Kalamata olives, sliced
1 cup chopped romaine lettuce	½ cup feta cheese, crumbled
2 tbsp extra virgin olive oil	1 tbsp red wine vinegar
1 tsp dried oregano	Salt and pepper to taste

Directions:

(1) Toss together romaine lettuce, cherry tomatoes, cucumber, red onion, and olives in a big bowl. *(2)* Top with the crumbled feta. *(3)* Combine the oregano, salt, pepper, red wine vinegar, olive oil, and a small bowl and whisk to combine. *(4)* Mix the salad ingredients by drizzling the dressing over it. *(5)* Quickly prepare and enjoy!

26. LOW-CARB CHICKEN CORDON BLEU

Total Time: 35 minutes | Prep Time: 10 minutes | Cook Time: 25 minutes

Ingredients:

2 boneless, skinless chicken breasts	4 slices ham
4 slices Swiss cheese	½ cup almond flour
1 egg, beaten	½ tsp garlic powder
½ tsp smoked paprika	½ tsp salt
½ tsp black pepper	1 tbsp olive oil

Directions:

(1) Get your oven preheated to 375°F, which is 190°C. **(2)** Cut the chicken breasts horizontally in half, being careful not to cut through. This will create a butterfly shape. **(3)** After stuffing two chicken breasts with ham and Swiss cheese, fold them back together. **(4)** The almond flour, garlic powder, paprika, salt, and pepper should be combined in a basin. **(5)** Coat the chicken breasts with the almond flour mixture after dipping them in the beaten egg. **(6)** The olive oil should be heated in a pan over medium-high heat. 4. Brown the chicken on both sides for about 2 minutes in total. **(7)** Take the chicken out of the oven and set it on a baking sheet after 20 minutes or when its internal temperature reaches 165°F or 74°C. **(8)** After a few minutes, set aside to relax.

27. CAULIFLOWER MASHED "POTATOES"

Total Time: 20 minutes | Prep Time: 10 minutes | Cook Time: 10 minutes

Ingredients:

1 medium head cauliflower, cut into florets	2 tbsp butter
¼ cup heavy cream	2 cloves garlic, minced
¼ cup grated Parmesan cheese	Salt and pepper to taste
1 tbsp chopped fresh chives (optional)	

Directions:

(1) Heat salted water in a saucepan and bring to a boil. Stir in the cauliflower florets and continue cooking for another 8 to 10 minutes or until they are soft to the bite. **(2)** Fill a food processor with the drained cauliflower. **(3)** Cream, butter, garlic, and Parmesan cheese should be added. Mix until combined. **(4)** To taste, season with salt and pepper. **(5)** Before serving, reheat the meal and garnish with chopped fresh chives, if desired.

28. SAUSAGE AND KALE SOUP

Total Time: 40 minutes | Prep Time: 10 minutes | Cook Time: 30 minutes

Ingredients:

1 lb Italian sausage (mild or spicy), casing removed	1 small onion, diced
2 cloves garlic, minced	4 cups chicken broth
1 cup heavy cream	3 cups chopped kale
1 medium zucchini, diced	1 tsp dried thyme
½ tsp salt	½ tsp black pepper
½ tsp red pepper flakes (optional)	

Directions:

(1) Sausage, crumbled, should be cooked in a big skillet over medium heat until browned. **(2)** Simmer for two or three minutes to soften the garlic and onion. **(3)** Simmer after adding the chicken broth. **(4)** Combine the zucchini, thyme, salt, pepper, and, if desired, red pepper flakes. Toss to combine. Let it simmer for ten minutes. *(5)* Chopped kale and heavy cream should be added. Once the kale begins to wilt, stir it and continue cooking for another 5 minutes. *(6)* Enjoy while hot!

29. CAULIFLOWER GNOCCHI WITH PESTO

Total Time: 30 minutes | Prep Time: 15 minutes | Cook Time: 15 minutes

Ingredients:

2 cups riced cauliflower	1 cup almond flour
½ cup grated Parmesan cheese	1 egg
½ tsp garlic powder	½ tsp salt
¼ tsp black pepper	1 tbsp olive oil
¼ cup pesto sauce	

Directions:

(1) After 5 minutes of steaming, drain the riced cauliflower using a clean kitchen towel. *(2)* The following ingredients should be mixed in a bowl: almond flour, cauliflower, Parmesan cheese, egg, garlic powder, salt, and black pepper. Blend ingredients until a dough is formed. *(3)* Split the dough in half and flatten out each half into a log. Slice into gnocchi-sized pieces, about 1 inch each. *(4)* Put a little oil in a skillet and place it on medium heat. Pour in the gnocchi and cook for two or three minutes on each side or until they get a golden brown color. *(5)* Before serving heat, toss the cooked gnocchi with the pesto sauce.

30. CUCUMBER AND AVOCADO GAZPACHO

Total Time: 10 minutes | Prep Time: 10 minutes

Ingredients:

1 large cucumber, peeled and chopped	1 ripe avocado, pitted and peeled
1 cup unsweetened coconut milk	½ cup fresh cilantro leaves
1 garlic clove, minced	2 tbsp lime juice
½ tsp sea salt	¼ tsp black pepper
½ cup cold water (adjust for consistency)	

Directions:

(1) A blender is the perfect tool for combining avocado, cucumber, coconut milk, cilantro, garlic, lime juice, salt, and pepper. Blend until smooth. *(2)* Add cold water gradually until the mixture reaches the required consistency, and blend until smooth. *(3)* Allow to chill for at least half an hour before consumption. *(4)* If preferred, serve chilled, garnish with more cilantro, and drizzle with olive oil.

31. LOW-CARB CLAM CHOWDER

Total Time: 35 minutes | Prep Time: 10 minutes

Ingredients:

2 tbsp butter	½ cup onion, diced
2 garlic cloves, minced	1 celery stalk, diced
1 cup cauliflower florets, chopped	1 cup unsweetened almond milk
1 cup heavy cream	1 can (6.5 oz) chopped clams, drained
½ tsp dried thyme	½ tsp sea salt
¼ tsp black pepper	2 tbsp fresh parsley, chopped

Directions:

(1) Butter should be heated in a big saucepan over medium heat. Saute the celery, garlic, and onion until they are tender. *(2)* Cook the cauliflower for a further 5 minutes after adding it. *(3)* Combine the almond milk and heavy cream by pouring them in while stirring. *(4)* Finish by adding the clams, thyme, salt, and pepper. The cauliflower should be

softened by simmering for 20 minutes. *(5)* To make the soup creamier, blend half of it and then add it back to the pot. *(6)* Prior to serving, top with chopped fresh parsley.

32. CREAMY SPINACH DIP

Total Time: 15 minutes | Prep Time: 10 minutes

Ingredients:

1 cup fresh spinach, finely chopped	½ cup Greek yogurt
¼ cup cream cheese softened	1 tbsp olive oil
1 garlic clove, minced	½ tsp onion powder
½ tsp sea salt	¼ tsp black pepper
1 tbsp lemon juice	

Directions:

(1) To get the best results, warm the olive oil in a skillet over medium heat. Toss in the garlic and sauté until it begins to smell good. *(2)* After around two minutes of stirring, the spinach should have wilted. Take it out of the oven. *(3)* Blend together the Greek yogurt, lime juice, cream cheese, salt, pepper, and sliced onion in a mixing bowl. Toss in the cooked spinach and mix well. *(4)* The low-carb crackers or vegetable sticks go well with it, whether it's warm or cooled.

33. ROASTED CABBAGE WEDGES

Total Time: 35 minutes | Prep Time: 5 minutes

Ingredients:

1 small cabbage, cut into wedges	2 tbsp olive oil
1 tsp garlic powder	½ tsp sea salt
¼ tsp black pepper	1 tsp smoked paprika
1 tbsp lemon juice	

Directions:

(1) Set oven temperature to 400°F. Sprinkle parchment paper on a baking pan. *(2)* Sprinkle the sheet with olive oil and arrange the cabbage slices on top. *(3)* Smoked paprika, salt, pepper, and garlic powder may be sprinkled over top. *(4)* To get crispy edges, roast for 30 minutes, turning once halfway through. *(5)* Serve with a drizzle of lemon juice.

34. ZESTY LEMON CHICKEN THIGHS

Total Time: 40 minutes | Prep Time: 10 minutes

Ingredients:

4 bone-in, skin-on chicken thighs	2 tbsp olive oil
2 tbsp lemon juice	1 tsp lemon zest
1 tsp garlic powder	½ tsp dried oregano
½ tsp sea salt	¼ tsp black pepper

Directions:

(1) Get your oven ready for 400°F or 200°C. *(2)* Add the olive oil, zest, lemon juice, garlic powder, oregano, salt, and pepper to a small bowl. *(3)* Spread the marinade evenly over the thighs of the chicken. *(4)* Place the chicken on a parchment-lined baking pan. *(5)* Crispy skin and an interior temperature of 165°F (74°C) are the results of 35 minutes in the oven. *(6)* Hot off the grill, top with roasted veggies or a crisp salad, and serve.

35. GARLIC PARMESAN CRUSTED PORK CHOPS

Total Time: 25 minutes | Prep Time: 10 minutes

Ingredients:

4 boneless pork chops	½ cup grated Parmesan cheese
½ teaspoon garlic powder	½ teaspoon onion powder
½ teaspoon smoked paprika	½ teaspoon salt
¼ teaspoon black pepper	1 tablespoon olive oil

Directions:

(1) Set oven temperature to 400°F. Sprinkle parchment paper on a baking pan. **(2)** Combine the flours of Parmesan, garlic, onion, paprika, salt, and pepper in a small bowl. **(3)** Before coating with the Parmesan mixture, brush each pork chop with olive oil. **(4)** Bake the pork chops for 15 to 18 minutes, or until they reach an internal temperature of 145°F or 63°C. **(5)** After 5 minutes, set aside to cool.

36. THAI PEANUT ZOODLE STIR-FRY

Total Time: 20 minutes | Prep Time: 10 minutes

Ingredients:

2 medium zucchinis, spiralized	1 tablespoon sesame oil
½ red bell pepper, thinly sliced	½ yellow bell pepper, thinly sliced
1 small carrot, julienned	1 clove garlic, minced
¼ cup peanut butter (sugar-free)	2 tablespoons soy sauce or coconut aminos
1 tablespoon rice vinegar	½ teaspoon ginger, grated
½ teaspoon red pepper flakes (optional)	¼ cup chopped peanuts, for garnish
2 tablespoons chopped cilantro for garnish	

Directions:

(1) In a big skillet, heat the sesame oil over medium heat. **(2)** Saute the garlic, carrots, and bell peppers for three to four minutes or until the peppers are just slightly softened. **(3)** Mix the garlic powder, salt, black pepper, olive oil, and shrimp together before coating. Stir to combine. Spiralize some zucchini and throw it in the pan with the other veggies. **(4)** Coat the zucchini noodles with the peanut sauce. Heat for 2 minutes or until done. **(5)** Take it off the stove and top it up with chopped cilantro and peanuts.

37. GARLIC BUTTER CHICKEN THIGHS

Total Time: 30 minutes | Prep Time: 10 minutes

Ingredients:

4 bone-in, skin-on chicken thighs	1 tablespoon olive oil
3 tablespoons unsalted butter	3 cloves garlic, minced
½ teaspoon salt	¼ teaspoon black pepper
½ teaspoon paprika	½ teaspoon dried thyme
½ teaspoon dried oregano	1 tablespoon fresh parsley, chopped

Directions:

(1) Get your oven preheated to 375°F, which is 190°C. **(2)** Rub paprika, salt, pepper, thyme, and oregano into chicken thighs. **(3)** In a big oven-safe skillet, heat the olive oil over medium-high heat. **(4)** Pound or sauté the chicken thighs for four to five minutes with the skin side down. After 2 minutes, turn over and sear the opposite side as well. **(5)** Lower the heat to medium and sauté the garlic and butter for one minute or until they release their aromatic scent. **(6)** For about fifteen to twenty minutes, or until a thermometer reads

165 degrees Fahrenheit (75 degrees Celsius), bake the chicken. Remove the pan from the oven. **(7)** Before serving hot, top with fresh parsley and a little garlic butter.

38. BUFFALO CAULIFLOWER TACOS

Total Time: 25 minutes | Prep Time: 10 minutes

Ingredients:

1 small head cauliflower, cut into florets	1 tablespoon olive oil
½ teaspoon garlic powder	½ teaspoon smoked paprika
¼ teaspoon salt	¼ cup buffalo sauce
4 small low-carb tortillas	¼ cup Greek yogurt or sour cream
1 tablespoon lime juice	¼ cup shredded lettuce
¼ cup diced tomatoes	2 tablespoons chopped cilantro

Directions:

(1) Roll out parchment paper and set the oven temperature to 400 degrees Fahrenheit. **(2)** Mix the paprika, garlic powder, olive oil, and salt with the cauliflower florets in a bowl. Prepare a baking sheet and coat it equally. **(3)** Cook, turning once, for fifteen minutes. **(4)** After 5 minutes, take the cauliflower out of the oven and coat it with buffalo sauce. **(5)** Greek yogurt and lime juice should be combined in a small dish. **(6)** Get the tacos ready: Spoon buffalo cauliflower, lettuce, and tomatoes onto tortillas; top with yogurt sauce. Season with cilantro and top with a dish.

39. LEMON PEPPER ZUCCHINI CHIPS

Total Time: 1 hour | Prep Time: 10 minutes

Ingredients:

2 medium zucchinis, thinly sliced	1 tablespoon olive oil
½ teaspoon sea sal	½ teaspoon black pepper
½ teaspoon lemon zest	¼ teaspoon garlic powder

Directions:

(1) Get your oven ready for 225°F (110°C) by preparing a baking sheet with parchment paper. Marinate the sliced zucchini in a big basin with olive oil, black pepper, garlic powder, lemon zest, and sea salt. **(2)** Put the slices on the baking sheet and spread them out in a single layer. **(3)** Chips should be crispy after 45 to 50 minutes in the oven, with a turn halfway through. **(4)** Let them cool down before you eat them. Snack on these crunchy, low-carb favorites!

40. ROASTED EGGPLANT DIP

Total Time: 45 minutes | Prep Time: 10 minutes

Ingredients:

1 large eggplant	2 tablespoons olive oil
1 garlic clove, minced	1 tablespoon lemon juice
½ teaspoon sea salt	¼ teaspoon black pepper
¼ teaspoon smoked paprika	2 tablespoons tahini (optional)
Fresh parsley for garnish	

Directions:

(1) Set the oven temperature to 400°F. After halving the eggplant lengthwise, drizzle one tablespoon of olive oil over each half. **(2)** After 25 to 30 minutes of roasting, turn the eggplant halves over and continue cooking until they are tender. **(3)** After the eggplant has cooled a little, remove its flesh and set it aside in a basin. *(4)* Proceed by adding the rest of the olive oil, garlic, lemon juice, salt, pepper, smoked paprika, and tahini (if desired). Puree or mix until combined. *(5)* Accompany it with veggie sticks or whole-grain crackers, and top it with fresh parsley.

41. ZOODLE AND MEATBALL MARINARA

Total Time: 30 minutes | Prep Time: 15 minutes

Ingredients:

For the Meatballs:

- 1 pound lean ground turkey or chicken
- 1 egg
- ½ teaspoon garlic powder
- ¼ teaspoon black pepper
- ¼ cup almond flour
- 1 teaspoon Italian seasoning
- ½ teaspoon sea salt

For the Marinara & Zoodles:

- 2 medium zucchini, spiralized into noodles
- 1 tablespoon olive oil
- 2 tablespoons grated Parmesan (optional)
- 1 cup sugar-free marinara sauce
- ¼ teaspoon red pepper flakes (optional)

Directions:

(1) To begin, set a baking sheet in a preheated oven to 375 degrees Fahrenheit and set a baking rack on top. Egg, almond flour, ground turkey, Italian seasoning, garlic powder, salt, and pepper should all be combined in a bowl. Roll into little meatballs. *(2)* Cook the meatballs, uncovered, for 15 to 18 minutes on the preheated baking sheet. *(3)* The oil for the pan should be heated over medium heat at the same time. Saute the zoodles for two or three minutes after adding them to the pan. *(4)* Put the cooked meatballs and marinara sauce in the pan. Cook, stirring occasionally, for 5 minutes. *(5)* When ready to serve, top with Parmesan and, if preferred, red pepper flakes.

42. GRILLED SHRIMP CAESAR SALAD

Total Time: 20 minutes | Prep Time: 10 minutes

Ingredients:

- 1 pound shrimp, peeled and deveined
- ½ teaspoon sea salt
- 1 teaspoon garlic powder
- ¼ cup grated Parmesan cheese
- ½ teaspoon lemon juice
- 1 tablespoon olive oil
- ¼ teaspoon black pepper
- 6 cups chopped Romaine lettuce
- ¼ cup Greek yogurt-based Caesar dressing
- ¼ cup crushed almonds or sunflower seeds (for crunch)

Directions:

(1) Bring a grill pan or grill out to medium heat. Mix the garlic powder, salt, black pepper, olive oil, and shrimp together before coating. *(2)* To make the shrimp opaque and pink, grill them for two to three minutes on each side. Take it out of the oven. *(3)* Salad greens, Parmesan, and Caesar dressing should be mixed in a big basin. Gently mix. *(4)* Top with grilled shrimp and lemon juice. *(5)* For a different texture, you may add crushed almonds or sunflower seeds. Make sure to serve right away.

43. GRILLED TERIYAKI SALMON

Total Time: 25 minutes | Prep Time: 10 minutes

Ingredients:

4 salmon fillets	¼ cup low-sodium soy sauce
2 tbsp sugar-free teriyaki sauce	1 tbsp olive oil
1 tbsp fresh ginger, grated	2 cloves garlic, minced
1 tsp sesame oil	1 tbsp sesame seeds (optional)
2 green onions, sliced	

Directions:

(1) Garlic, ginger, sesame oil, olive oil, soy sauce, and teriyaki sauce should all be combined in a small bowl. Fill a shallow dish with the marinade and pour it over the salmon fillets. **(2)** Let it sit in the marinade for at least 10 minutes. **(3)** Get the grill ready by heating it to medium. **(4)** To make sure the salmon flakes readily when tested with a fork, grill it for four to five minutes on each side. **(5)** Add some green onions and sesame seeds as a garnish before serving. Tuck into it!

44. AVOCADO TUNA SALAD

Total Time: 10 minutes | Prep Time: 10 minutes

Ingredients:

2 cans of tuna in water	1 large ripe avocado, mashed
¼ cup red onion, finely chopped	½ cup cucumber, diced
1 tbsp lemon juice	1 tbsp fresh parsley, chopped
½ tsp salt	¼ tsp black pepper
¼ tsp garlic powder	

Directions:

(1) Mix the avocado mashed with the tuna in a big basin. **(2)** Stir in the chopped red onion, cucumber, lemon zest, parsley, season with salt and pepper, then stir in the garlic powder. **(3)** Thoroughly blend all ingredients. **(4)** Over lettuce wraps, over whole grain bread, or by itself—it's delicious anyway.

45. LEMON DILL BAKED COD

Total Time: 20 minutes | Prep Time: 5 minutes

Ingredients:

4 cod fillets	2 tbsp olive oil
2 tbsp lemon juice	1 tsp lemon zest
1 tbsp fresh dill, chopped	2 cloves garlic, minced
½ tsp salt	¼ tsp black pepper

Directions:

(1) Set oven temperature to 400°F. Sprinkle parchment paper on a baking pan. **(2)** Once the baking sheet is ready, lay the fish fillets on top. **(3)** In a delicate bowl, mix together the olive oil and juice from the zest of the lemon, dill, garlic, salt, and black pepper. Coat the fish fillets with the mixture using a brush. **(4)** To make sure the fish flakes readily when tested with a fork, bake it for 12–15 minutes. **(5)** With a side of fresh salad or steaming veggies, serve warm.

46. CAULIFLOWER PIZZA BITES

Total Time: 35 minutes | Prep Time: 15 minutes

Ingredients:

2 cups cauliflower rice (fresh or frozen)	1 large egg, beaten
½ cup shredded mozzarella cheese	¼ cup grated Parmesan chees

½ tsp Italian seasoning	¼ tsp garlic powder
¼ tsp salt	¼ tsp black pepper
½ cup sugar-free marinara sauce	¼ cup mini turkey pepperoni (optional)

Directions:

(1) Get your oven preheated to 375°F, which is 190°C. Sprinkle parchment paper on a baking pan. **(2)** Drain any extra liquid and microwave the cauliflower rice for three minutes if it is frozen. **(3)** In a bowl, combine the garlic powder, egg, mozzarella, Parmesan, cauliflower rice, Italian seasoning, salt, and black pepper. Add the Italian seasoning and combine well. Roll out little scoops of the mixture into bite-sized balls. **(4)** After 20 minutes in the oven, the top should be golden brown. **(5)** After 5 minutes, take it out and sprinkle turkey pepperoni and marinara sauce over top. **(6)** Warm it up and savor it!

47. ZUCCHINI AND TURKEY SKILLET

Total Time: 25 minutes | Prep Time: 10 minutes

Ingredients:

1 lb ground turkey	2 medium zucchinis, diced
1 small onion, chopped	2 cloves garlic, minced
1 cup cherry tomatoes, halved	1 tsp olive oil
1/2 tsp paprika	1/2 tsp dried oregano
1/2 tsp salt	1/4 tsp black pepper
1/4 tsp red pepper flakes (optional)	1/4 cup grated Parmesan cheese (optional)

Directions:

(1) Spread out the olive oil and set it over medium heat in a large pan. Sauté the garlic and onion for 2 minutes or until they release their aroma. **(2)** The ground turkey should be browned and sautéed for about 5 minutes, stirring occasionally with a spatula. Chop some cherry tomatoes and zucchini and add them together with some paprika, oregano, salt, black pepper, and red pepper flakes. **(3)** Mix well. To get soft zucchini, cook for an additional 5 to 7 minutes. **(4)** Take it off the stove and, if you're using it, top it with Parmesan. **(5)** Enjoy while hot!

48. MEDITERRANEAN STUFFED BELL PEPPERS

Total Time: 40 minutes | Prep Time: 15 minutes

Ingredients:

4 large bell peppers (any color), halved	1 lb ground chicken or turkey
1 small onion, chopped	2 cloves garlic, minced
1 small zucchini, diced	1/2 cup diced tomatoes
1/4 cup feta cheese, crumbled	1 tsp olive oil
1 tsp dried oregano	1/2 tsp cumin
1/2 tsp salt	1/4 tsp black pepper

Directions:

(1) Get your oven preheated to 375°F, which is 190°C. **(2)** Put a little oil in a skillet and place it on medium heat. Sauté the garlic and onion for 2 minutes. **(3)** Brown the ground turkey or chicken, which should take around 5 minutes. **(4)** Zucchini, tomato dice, cumin, oregano, salt, and pepper should be stirred in. Remove from heat and let sit for three minutes. **(5)** Split the bell peppers in half and spoon the mixture into each half. **(6)** Twenty minutes in the oven should do the trick for stuffing peppers. **(7)** After 5 minutes, take out of the oven and top with feta cheese. **(8)** Warm it up and savor it!

49. LOW-CARB SHRIMP FAJITAS

Total Time: 20 minutes | Prep Time: 10 minutes

Ingredients:

1 lb shrimp, peeled and deveined	1 red bell pepper, sliced
1 yellow bell pepper, sliced	1 small red onion, sliced
1 tbsp olive oil	1 tsp chili powder
1/2 tsp cumin	1/2 tsp smoked paprika
1/2 tsp garlic powder	1/2 tsp salt
1/4 tsp black pepper	1 tbsp lime juice
1/4 cup fresh cilantro, chopped	

Directions:

(1) Toss the olive oil into a large pan and heat it over medium-high heat. Sauté the onions and bell peppers for three to four minutes or until they are just barely softened. **(2)** Toss in the shrimp along with the black pepper, cumin, garlic powder, paprika, and chili powder. Keep cooking for another three to four minutes or until shrimp become opaque and pink. **(3)** Add fresh cilantro and squeeze some lime juice on top. **(4)** Garnish with low-carb tortillas or lettuce wraps. Savor it!

50. LOW-CARB CHICKEN TIKKA MASALA

Total Time: 30 minutes | Prep Time: 10 minutes

Ingredients:

1 lb boneless, skinless chicken breast	1/2 cup plain Greek yogurt
1 tbsp lemon juice	1 tsp garam masala
1/2 tsp turmeric	1/2 tsp cumin
1/2 tsp salt	1/4 tsp black pepper
1 tbsp olive oil	1 small onion, chopped
2 cloves garlic, minced	1 tsp grated ginger
1 cup diced tomatoes	1/2 cup coconut milk
1/2 tsp paprika	1/4 tsp cayenne pepper (optional)
2 tbsp fresh cilantro, chopped	

Directions:

(1) Combine the Greek yogurt, lemon juice, cumin, turmeric, salt, and black pepper in a bowl. Add the garam masala and stir well. Marinate the chicken for 10 minutes after adding it. **(2)** Toss the olive oil in a pan and heat it up over medium heat. Saute the garlic, ginger, and onion well. Keep cooking for another minute. **(3)** Once the chicken has marinated, add it to the pan and brown it for 5 to 6 minutes. **(4)** Pour in the coconut milk, paprika, chopped tomatoes, and cayenne pepper (if desired). Reduce heat & simmer for ten minutes or until the chicken is done. **(5)** Serve with low-carb side dishes or cauliflower rice and top with fresh cilantro for a garnish.

51. CAULIFLOWER HUMMUS

Total Time: 25 minutes | Prep Time: 10 minutes | Cook Time: 15 minutes

Ingredients:

1 small head cauliflower, cut into florets	2 tbsp olive oil
2 cloves garlic, minced	¼ cup tahini
2 tbsp lemon juice	½ tsp ground cumin
½ tsp salt	¼ tsp paprika (for garnish)
2 tbsp water (if needed for consistency)	

Directions:

(1) Set the oven heat to 400°F. Sprinkle parchment paper on a baking pan. (2) Mix the cauliflower florets in a single tablespoon of olive oil. Roast for fifteen minutes or until tender. Fill a food processor with the roasted cauliflower. Combine the remaining olive oil, garlic, tahini, lemon juice, cumin, and salt. (3) Add water as required to blend until smooth or consistency is reached. (4) Before serving, transfer to a plate and top with paprika. Accompany with crisp vegetables and low-carb crackers.

52. CREAMY ROASTED RED PEPPER SOUP

Total Time: 30 minutes | Prep Time: 10 minutes | Cook Time: 20 minutes

Ingredients:

2 large red bell peppers, roasted, peeled	1 tbsp olive oil
1 small onion, chopped	2 cloves garlic, minced
2 cups low-sodium vegetable broth	1 tsp smoked paprika
½ tsp salt	¼ tsp black pepper
½ cup unsweetened coconut milk	

Directions:

(1) Put the olive oil in a pot and place it over medium heat. Sauté the chopped onion for about three minutes or until it becomes tender. (2) Cook, stirring occasionally, for 30 more seconds or until the garlic is aromatic. (3) Once the stock is boiling, add the smoked paprika, roasted red bell peppers, and salt and pepper to taste. Stir to combine. Cook, covered, at a low simmer for 10 minutes. (4) Smooth up the soup by blending it with an immersion blender or, alternatively, by gently transferring it to a blender. (5) After five further minutes of simmering, stir in the coconut milk. Modify seasoning as necessary. (6) Top with chopped fresh herbs or a splash of coconut milk, and serve hot.

53. GARLIC HERB ZUCCHINI CHIPS

Total Time: 2 hours | Prep Time: 10 minutes | Cook Time: 1 hour 50 minutes

Ingredients:

2 medium zucchinis, thinly sliced	1 tbsp olive oil
½ tsp garlic powder	½ tsp dried oregano
½ tsp dried basil	½ tsp salt
¼ tsp black pepper	

Directions:

(1) The oven should be preheated to 225°F, also known as 110°C. Sprinkle parchment paper on a baking pan. (2) Combine the garlic powder, olive oil, oregano, basil, salt, and pepper in a bowl, and then toss in the zucchini slices. (3) Lay down the zucchini slices one layer on top of the baking sheet that you just prepared. (4) To get crispy, bake for 1 hour and 50 minutes, turning once halfway through. (5) Let it cool a little bit before you eat it. Seal any leftover food and store it in the fridge.

54. SPAGHETTI SQUASH PAD THAI

Total Time: 40 minutes | Prep Time: 10 minutes | Cook Time: 30 minutes

Ingredients:

1 medium spaghetti squash	1 tbsp olive oil
2 cloves garlic, minced	1 small onion, chopped
1 cup shredded	1 red bell pepper,

carrots	sliced
½ cup shredded cabbage	1 egg, lightly beaten
½ cup cooked chicken or shrimp (optional)	¼ cup chopped peanuts (for garnish)
2 tbsp chopped green onions	For the Sauce:
3 tbsp tamari or coconut aminos	1 tbsp lime juice
1 tbsp almond butter or peanut butter	½ tsp sriracha (optional)

Directions:

(1) Set the oven temperature to 400°F. Peel the spaghetti squash, cut it in half, and roast it face down for 25-30 minutes after removing the seeds. **(2)** Use a fork to extract any strings from the squash as it cools. To get the best results, warm the olive oil in a skillet over medium heat. For two minutes, sauté the onion and garlic. **(3)** Incorporate cabbage, bell pepper, and carrots. Gently simmer for three to four minutes or until the vegetable is soft. **(4)** Toss the vegetables to the side and scramble the eggs in the pan. **(5)** Toss in the spaghetti squash strands and, if desired, cooked shrimp or chicken. **(6)** Use a fork to extract any strings from the squash as it cools. Coat the squash mixture by pouring it over it and stirring. **(7)** Add some chopped peanuts and green onions as a garnish. Keep heated before serving.

55. GRILLED STEAK WITH CAULIFLOWER MASH

Total Time: 30 minutes | Prep Time: 10 minutes

Ingredients:

2 (6-ounce) lean sirloin steaks	1 teaspoon olive oil
½ teaspoon salt	½ teaspoon black pepper
1 teaspoon garlic powder	1 teaspoon dried rosemary
1 small head cauliflower, chopped	2 tablespoons unsweetened almond milk
1 tablespoon butter	1 teaspoon minced garlic

Directions:

(1) Warm up the grill to a medium-high temperature. **(2)** Marinate the steaks in a mixture of rosemary, garlic powder, salt, and black pepper. **(3)** Sear the steaks for four to five minutes on each side or until done to your liking. After 5 minutes, set aside. **(4)** Ten minutes into the steaming process, the cauliflower should be tender. **(5)** The steamed cauliflower should be transferred to a food processor. Include the butter, almond milk, and garlic. Mix until combined. **(6)** Accompany the grilled steak with mashed cauliflower.

56. ROASTED CAULIFLOWER STEAK

Total Time: 35 minutes | Prep Time: 10 minutes

Ingredients:

one large head of cauliflower sliced into thick steaks	2 tablespoons olive oil
½ teaspoon salt	½ teaspoon black pepper
1 teaspoon smoked paprika	½ teaspoon garlic powder
½ teaspoon onion powder	1 teaspoon lemon juice

Directions:

(1) Set oven temperature to 400°F. Sprinkle parchment paper on a baking pan. **(2)** Preheat a baking sheet and lay out the cauliflower steaks. Put a little olive oil on top. **(3)** Onion powder, smoked paprika, salt, pepper, and garlic powder may be sprinkled over top. *(4)* Cook, turning once halfway through, for 25 to 30 minutes or until browned and soft. *(5)* Serve with a drizzle of lemon juice.

57. SLOW-COOKER LEMON HERB CHICKEN

Total Time: 6 hours | Prep Time: 10 minutes

Ingredients:

2 boneless, skinless chicken breasts	1 teaspoon salt
½ teaspoon black pepper	1 teaspoon dried thyme
1 teaspoon dried oregano	1 teaspoon garlic powder
½ teaspoon onion powder	½ cup low-sodium chicken broth
Juice of 1 lemon	1 tablespoon olive oil

Directions:

(1) Simmer the chicken breasts for a few hours. *(2)* Add chili powder, onion powder, garlic powder, thyme, oregano, and salt & pepper to taste. *(3)* Add the chicken broth & squeeze in the lemon juice. Put a little olive oil on top. *(4)* When the chicken reaches the desired doneness, cover and simmer for 6 hours (or 3 hours on high). *(5)* Use the slow cooker liquids to shred or serve whole.

58. GARLIC ROASTED BRUSSELS SPROUTS

Total Time: 25 minutes | Prep Time: 5 minutes

Ingredients:

1 pound Brussels sprouts, trimmed and halved	2 tablespoons olive oil
1 teaspoon salt	½ teaspoon black pepper
1 teaspoon garlic powder	½ teaspoon crushed red pepper flakes (optional)

Directions:

(1) Set oven heat to 400°F. *(2)* Salted, peppered, garlic powdered, and flecked with red pepper, toss the Brussels sprouts with the olive oil. *(3)* Arrange in a uniform layer on a baking pan. *(4)* Cook, stirring halfway through, for 20 to 25 minutes or until crisp and golden brown. *(5)* Keep heated before serving.

59. GARLIC BUTTER BAKED SALMON

Total Time: 25 minutes | Prep Time: 10 minutes

Ingredients:

2 salmon fillets (6 oz each)	2 tbsp unsalted butter, melted
2 cloves garlic, minced	1 tbsp lemon juice
1 tsp dried oregano	½ tsp salt
½ tsp black pepper	½ tsp paprika
1 tbsp chopped fresh parsley (for garnish)	Lemon wedges (for serving)

Directions:

(1) Set oven temperature to 375°F. Sprinkle parchment paper on a baking pan. *(2)* In a little dish, combine the paprika, salt, pepper, oregano, lemon juice, garlic, and melted butter. *(3)* Spread the garlic butter blend evenly over the baking sheet and coat the salmon fillets. *(4)* The salmon should be opaque and flaky after 15 to 18 minutes in the oven. *(5)* The addition of fresh parsley and lemon wedges makes for a lovely garnish.

60. PESTO GRILLED SHRIMP

Total Time: 20 minutes | Prep Time: 10 minutes

Ingredients:

1 lb large shrimp, peeled and deveined	¼ cup basil pesto (store-bought or homemade)
1 tbsp olive oil	½ tsp salt
½ tsp black pepper	½ tsp red pepper flakes (optional)
1 tbsp lemon juice	

Directions:

(1) Pesto, olive oil, salt, pepper, and red pepper flakes should be mixed with the shrimp in a dish. Spend 10 minutes letting it marinate. **(2)** Get a grill or pan ready by heating it up over medium-high heat. **(3)** To make the shrimp opaque and pink, thread them onto skewers and cook for two to three minutes on each side. **(4)** Serve with a drizzle of lemon juice.

61. THAI COCONUT SHRIMP SOUP

Total Time: 30 minutes | Prep Time: 10 minutes

Ingredients:

1 tbsp coconut oil	1 small onion, diced
2 cloves garlic, minced	1-inch ginger, grated
1 tbsp red curry paste	4 cups low-sodium chicken or vegetable broth
1 can (13.5 oz) coconut milk	1 tbsp fish sauce
1 tbsp lime juice	½ tsp salt
½ tsp black pepper	1 lb shrimp, peeled and deveined
1 cup sliced mushrooms	½ cup red bell pepper, sliced
¼ cup chopped fresh cilantro	

Directions:

(1) Melt the coconut oil in a pot set over medium heat. For two minutes, sauté the ginger, garlic, and onion. **(2)** Add the red curry paste & continue cooking for one more minute. **(3)** Spice it up with some salt, pepper, lime juice, fish sauce, coconut milk, and broth. Heat till simmering. **(4)** Incorporate the bell pepper, shrimp, and mushrooms. To get thoroughly cooked, pink shrimp is heated for 5 to 7 minutes. **(5)** Serve with a sprinkle of fresh cilantro as a garnish.

62. AVOCADO CHOCOLATE SMOOTHIE

Total Time: 5 minutes | Prep Time: 5 minutes

Ingredients:

1 ripe avocado	1 cup unsweetened almond milk
1 tbsp unsweetened cocoa powder	1 tbsp chia seeds
½ tsp vanilla extract	1 tbsp sugar-free sweetener (monk fruit or stevia)
½ cup ice cubes	

Directions:

(1) Blend all the ingredients together. **(2)** Whisk or mix until combined. **(3)** Serve immediately after pouring into a glass.

63. TURKEY TACO LETTUCE CUPS

Total Time: 20 minutes | Prep Time: 10 minutes

Ingredients:

1 lb ground turkey	1 tbsp olive oil
1 tsp cumin	1 tsp chili powder
½ tsp garlic powder	½ tsp onion powder
½ tsp smoked paprika	¼ tsp salt
¼ tsp black pepper	½ cup diced tomatoes
¼ cup chopped cilantro	8 large lettuce leaves (romaine or butter lettuce)

½ cup shredded cheese (optional)	½ avocado, diced
¼ cup plain Greek yogurt (for topping)	

Directions:

(1) Heat a skillet over medium heat and add a little oil. Toss the turkey in the ground and brown it while stirring occasionally. *(2)* Powdered garlic, onion, cumin, chile, paprika, salt, and black pepper should be added. Be sure to mix well. *(3)* Cook for a further 2 minutes after adding the diced tomatoes. *(4)* Stir in the chopped cilantro after removing from the heat. *(5)* Fill lettuce leaves with turkey mixture and spoon it on top. *(6)* If desired, garnish with shredded cheese, chopped avocado, and Greek yogurt. Make sure to serve right away.

64. DILL LEMON CHICKEN SALAD

Total Time: 15 minutes | Prep Time: 10 minutes

Ingredients:

2 cups cooked and shredded chicken breast	½ cup plain Greek yogurt
1 tbsp mayonnaise (optional)	1 tbsp fresh lemon juice
1 tsp lemon zest	1 tbsp fresh dill, chopped
½ tsp garlic powder	½ tsp salt
¼ tsp black pepper	½ cup diced celery
¼ cup chopped red onion	½ avocado, diced (optional)

Directions:

(1) Gather all the ingredients in a big bowl. Those who want it with a little more flavor may add Greek yogurt, dill, garlic powder, salt, and black pepper. Thoroughly blend. *(2)* Toss in some red onion, celery, and shredded chicken. Combine and coat. *(3)* Add diced avocado, if using, and gently mix. *(4)* Present chilled, on whole-grain crackers, in a lettuce wrap, or on a bed of greens.

65. ZOODLE ALFREDO WITH CHICKEN

Total Time: 25 minutes | Prep Time: 10 minutes

Ingredients:

2 medium zucchini, spiralized into zoodles	1 tbsp olive oil
1 lb boneless, skinless chicken breast, diced	2 cloves garlic, minced
½ cup heavy cream	¼ cup grated Parmesan cheese
¼ tsp salt	¼ tsp black pepper
½ tsp Italian seasoning	1 tbsp butte
½ cup baby spinach (optional)	1 tbsp chopped fresh parsley (for garnish)

Directions:

(1) Spread out the olive oil and set it over medium heat in a large pan. After a few minutes, add the diced chicken and cook until it's thoroughly cooked and has a golden brown color. Take off the pan and put aside. *(2)* While the butter is melting, sauté the minced garlic for one minute in the same pan. *(3)* Incorporate the Parmesan cheese and heavy cream after seasoning with salt, pepper, and Italian seasoning. Allow to simmer for a duration of 2 minutes. *(4)* Stir in the zoodles and sauté for two or three minutes or until they are barely cooked. *(5)* Add the cooked chicken and, if desired, the baby spinach. Gently mix. *(6)* Take it off the stove and top it up with some fresh parsley. Make the serving right away.

66. CABBAGE SLAW WITH CILANTRO DRESSING

Total Time: 15 minutes | Prep Time: 10 minutes

Ingredients:

- 3 cups shredded green cabbage
- 1 cup shredded carrots
- ¼ cup sliced green onions
- 1 cup shredded purple cabbage
- ½ cup chopped cilantro
- ¼ cup toasted pumpkin seeds (optional)

For the Dressing:
- 2 tbsp fresh lime juice
- ½ tsp honey or sugar substitute
- 1 small garlic clove, minced
- ¼ tsp black pepper
- 3 tbsp olive oil
- 1 tbsp apple cider vinegar
- 1 tsp Dijon mustard
- ½ tsp salt

Directions:

(1) Toss the olive oil, lime juice, apple cider vinegar, honey, Dijon mustard, garlic, salt, and pepper in a small bowl. Whisk to combine. Remove off the table. **(2)** Toss together the green and purple cabbages, carrots, cilantro, and green onions in a large basin. **(3)** Add the vinaigrette and mix the slaw well. **(4)** If you'd like, you may top it with toasted pumpkin seeds. Permit flavors to combine by letting it rest for 5–10 minutes before serving.

67. ROASTED GARLIC CAULIFLOWER SOUP

Total Time: 40 minutes | Prep Time: 10 minutes | Cook Time: 30 minutes | Servings: 4

Ingredients:

- one large head of cauliflower
- 2 tablespoons olive oil
- 4 cups low-sodium vegetable broth
- 1 teaspoon dried thyme
- 1/4 teaspoon ground black pepper
- 1 whole garlic bulb
- 1 small onion, chopped
- 1/2 cup unsweetened almond milk
- 1/2 teaspoon sea salt
- Optional garnish: fresh parsley, a drizzle of olive oil

Directions:

(1) Set the oven temperature to 400°F. **(2)** Peel and mince the garlic: Remove the garlic bulb's top and cut it open to reveal the cloves. Before placing it on a baking pan, coat it with one teaspoon of olive oil, then cover it in foil. **(3)** Put the garlic cloves and cauliflower florets in the oven at the same time. Before roasting for 25-30 minutes, drizzle with one tablespoon of olive oil. Cook until brown and soft. **(4)** Over medium heat, sauté the onion for around 5 minutes in the remaining olive oil in a large saucepan until it becomes translucent. **(5)** While the cauliflower is roasting, add it to the saucepan. After the garlic cloves have roasted, remove their skins and add them to the mixture. **(6)** Add the thyme, salt, pepper, and vegetable broth. Cook, covered, over low heat for ten minutes. **(7)** Make sure the soup is smooth by blending it with an immersion blender. Before serving, taste and add almond milk; season to taste. **(8)** Warm the dish and top it with chopped parsley or a little olive oil before serving.

68. LOW-CARB MEATBALL ZOODLES

Total Time: 35 minutes | Prep Time: 15 minutes | Cook Time: 20 minutes | Servings: 4

Ingredients:

For the Meatballs:

1 lb ground turkey or chicken
1 large egg
1 tablespoon fresh parsley, chopped
1/2 teaspoon sea salt
1/4 cup almond flour
2 cloves garlic, minced
1/2 teaspoon dried oregano
1/4 teaspoon black pepper

For the Zoodles:

4 medium zucchinis, spiralized
1 cup sugar-free marinara sauce
Fresh basil for garnish
2 tablespoons olive oil
1/4 teaspoon red pepper flakes (optional)

Directions:

(1) Set oven temperature to 375°F. *(2)* Get the meatballs started: Mix together the almond flour, ground turkey, egg, garlic, parsley, oregano, salt, and pepper in a big basin. Blend just until barely mixed. Make balls that are one inch in diameter. *(3)* The meatballs should be cooked and browned after 18 to 20 minutes in the oven on a baking sheet coated with parchment paper. *(4)* Chop and wash the zoodles. Spread out the olive oil and set it over medium heat in a large pan. Toss in the spiralized zucchini and cook for two or three minutes or until just softened but not mushy. *(5)* Reduce the heat to medium-low and warm the marinara sauce in a small saucepan. If you like, you may add red pepper flakes. *(6)* Step 1: Combine the meatballs and zoodles in a pan. Second Step: Top with the sauce. Step 3: Gently stir to combine. *(7)* Serve immediately after garnishing with fresh basil.

69. TUSCAN KALE AND SAUSAGE SOUP

Total Time: 40 minutes | Prep Time: 10 minutes | Cook Time: 30 minutes | Servings: 4

Ingredients:

1 tablespoon olive oil
1 small onion, diced
4 cups low-sodium chicken broth
1 head of cauliflower, cut into small florets
1/2 teaspoon dried thyme
1/4 teaspoon crushed red pepper flakes
Fresh parsley for garnish
1 lb Italian chicken sausage (casing removed, crumbled)
3 cloves garlic, minced
1 cup unsweetened almond milk
4 cups chopped kale, ribs removed
1/2 teaspoon dried oregano
Salt and pepper to taste

Directions:

(1) The best way to heat olive oil is in a large pot over medium heat. Toss in the crumbled sausage and brown it for another 5 to 6 minutes. *(2)* Put the garlic and onion in the saucepan. Cook for about three minutes or until the mixture is aromatic and slightly thickened. *(3)* Add the almond milk and chicken broth. Combine by stirring. *(4)* Throw in some thyme, oregano, red pepper flakes, and cauliflower florets. To make the cauliflower soft, simmer for around 15 minutes. *(5)* After 5 minutes, add the chopped kale and continue cooking until the kale wilts. *(6)* Add salt and pepper to taste. *(7)* Top with freshly chopped parsley and serve while still hot.

70. LOW-CARB PHILLY CHEESESTEAK SKILLET

Total Time: 30 minutes | Prep Time: 10 minutes | Cook Time: 20 minutes | Servings: 4

Ingredients:

1 tablespoon olive oil
1 green bell pepper,
1 lb thinly sliced sirloin steak (or ribeye)
1 red bell pepper,

thinly sliced
1 small onion, thinly sliced
2 cloves garlic, minced
1/2 teaspoon sea salt
1/2 cup shredded provolone or mozzarella chees

thinly sliced
1 cup sliced mushrooms
1 teaspoon Worcestershire sauce
1/4 teaspoon black pepper
Optional: fresh parsley for garnish

Directions:

(1) Toss the olive oil into a large pan and heat it over medium-high heat. Cook the steak slices in a skillet. Just before it's done, sear for two to three minutes on each side. Detach and put aside. **(2)** Bell peppers, onions, and mushrooms should all be added to the same pan. Simmer, covered, for 5–6 minutes, or until almost done, or until heat is high. **(3)** Sauté the garlic for a further minute. **(4)** Once the meat has been removed from the pan, stir in the Worcestershire sauce and add salt and pepper. Heat through by tossing everything together and cooking for a further two or three minutes. **(5)** On top, crumble some cheese. Cook, covered, for about 2 minutes or until the cheese melts. **(6)** Warm it and top it with minced parsley if you want.

71. CREAMY BROCCOLI CAULIFLOWER CASSEROLE

Total Time: 40 minutes | Prep Time: 10 minutes | Cook Time: 30 minutes | Servings: 4

Ingredients:

2 cups broccoli florets
1 tablespoon olive oil
1/2 teaspoon onion powder
1/4 teaspoon black pepper
1/4 cup grated Parmesan cheese
1 tablespoon nutritional yeast (optional for a cheesy flavor boost)
2 tablespoons chopped fresh parsley

2 cups cauliflower florets
1/2 teaspoon garlic powder
1/2 teaspoon salt
1/2 cup plain Greek yogurt (unsweetened, low-fat)
1/2 cup shredded mozzarella cheese
1/4 cup unsweetened almond milk

Directions:

(1) Adjust the oven temperature to high (375°F, 190°C). Lightly coat a medium-sized casserole dish with cooking spray or olive oil. **(2)** Broccoli and cauliflower florets should be blanched or steam-cooked for three to four minutes or until crisp-tender. Reserve the drained liquid. **(3)** Lightly coat a medium-sized casserole dish with cooking spray or olive oil. Whisk to combine. **(4)** Once the broccoli and cauliflower have been cooked, add them to the yogurt mixture and stir until equally covered. **(5)** After the casserole dish is ready, transfer the mixture to it. Before serving, top with shredded mozzarella cheese. **(6)** Cook in the oven for twenty-five to thirty minutes or until the cheese is melted and bubbling and a little brown on top. **(7)** Once taken out of the oven, set aside to cool. Chopped parsley may be used as a garnish if preferred. **(8)** Warm it up before serving.

72. BAKED LEMON HERB SALMON

Total Time: 25 minutes | Prep Time: 10 minutes | Cook Time: 15 minutes | Servings: 4

Ingredients:

4 salmon fillets (about 4–5 oz each)
2 tablespoons fresh lemon juice

2 tablespoons olive oil
1 teaspoon lemon zest

1 teaspoon dried oregano
1/2 teaspoon garlic powder
1/4 teaspoon black pepper
Fresh parsley (optional, for garnish)

1 teaspoon dried parsley
1/2 teaspoon salt

Lemon wedges (for serving)

Directions:

(1) There is no way to avoid preheating the oven to 200°C (400°F). To get a baking sheet ready, grease it or line it with parchment paper. **(2)** For the dressing, combine the vinegar, olive oil, parsley, lemon juice and zest, oregano, garlic powder, salt, and pepper in a small bowl. **(3)** After preparing a baking sheet, lay the salmon fillets skin-side down. Coat the fillets evenly with the lemon-herb mixture. **(4)** When examined with a fork, the salmon should flake readily after 12–15 minutes in the oven. Take it out and set it aside to rest for two minutes. **(5)** If you'd like, you may top it up with some fresh parsley and serve it with lemon wedges.

73. CREAMY GARLIC SHRIMP AND SPINACH

Total Time: 20 minutes | Prep Time: 5 minutes | Cook Time: 15 minutes | Servings: 4

Ingredients:

1 pound large shrimp, peeled and deveined
4 cloves garlic, minced

1/2 cup plain Greek yogurt (unsweetened, low-fat)
2 tablespoons grated Parmesan cheese
1/2 teaspoon salt

1 tablespoon lemon juice

1 tablespoon olive oil

3 cups baby spinach leaves
1/4 cup unsweetened almond milk
1/2 teaspoon smoked paprika
1/4 teaspoon black pepper
Fresh parsley (optional, for garnish)

Directions:

(1) In a big skillet set over medium heat, warm the olive oil. When the garlic is aromatic, add the minced garlic and cook for another minute. **(2)** Then, toss in the shrimp. Sprinkle with pepper, salt, and paprika. Once the shrimp become pink and opaque, cook them for another two to three minutes on each side. **(3)** Before the baby spinach wilts, add it and simmer for another two minutes. **(4)** Turn the heat down to low. Whisk in the lemon juice, Parmesan cheese, almond milk, Greek yogurt, and almonds. To get a creamy, warmed sauce, continue cooking for an additional two to three minutes. **(5)** Reevaluate the seasoning according to your taste. **(6)** If you'd like, you may remove it from the heat and top it with chopped parsley. **(7)** If you want to make it a full Mounjaro-friendly dinner, you may serve it hot and top it with cauliflower rice or zucchini noodles.

74. ROASTED VEGGIE BUDDHA BOWL

Total Time: 40 minutes | Prep Time: 15 minutes | Cook Time: 25 minutes | Servings: 4

Ingredients:

For the Roasted Vegetables:

1 cup sweet potato, peeled and diced
1 cup cauliflower florets
1 zucchini, sliced
1 teaspoon garlic powder
1/2 teaspoon salt

1 cup broccoli florets
1 red bell pepper, sliced
2 tablespoons olive oil
1/2 teaspoon smoked paprika
1/4 teaspoon black pepper

For the Bowl Base & Toppings:

- 2 cups cooked quinoa or cauliflower rice
- 1 avocado, sliced
- 2 tablespoons tahini
- 1 tablespoon water
- 1/2 cup canned chickpeas, rinsed
- 2 tablespoons pumpkin seeds (optional)
- 1 tablespoon lemon juice
- Salt and pepper to taste

Directions:

(1) Preheating the oven to 400°F is not an option. On a large baking pan, lay down parchment paper. In a large basin, mix together the zucchini, sweet potato, broccoli, cauliflower, and red bell pepper. Add some seasonings, like garlic powder, smoked paprika, olive oil, and salt & pepper. Coat by tossing. **(2)** Ensure that the veggies are evenly distributed throughout the baking sheet. Soften and softly brown, about 25 to 30 minutes, rotating once. **(3)** Whisk the tahini dressing ingredients (tahini, water, lemon juice, salt, and pepper) until creamy while the veggies are roasting. To get the consistency you wish, add more water as necessary. **(4)** After the quinoa or cauliflower rice has cooked, divide it into four bowls and set them up. Divide the roasted vegetables among the plates and garnish with chickpeas, avocado slices, and pumpkin seeds, if desired. **(5)** Spoon the tahini sauce into each of the serving dishes. **(6)** Make sure to serve right away.

75. SPICY KOREAN CAULIFLOWER WINGS

Total Time: 40 minutes | Prep Time: 15 minutes | Cook Time: 25 minutes | Servings: 4

Ingredients:

- 1 medium head cauliflower, cut into florets
- 1/4 cup unsweetened almond milk
- 1 tablespoon olive oil
- 1 teaspoon paprika
- 1/4 teaspoon black pepper
- 2 tablespoons gochujang (Korean chili paste or sugar-free chili paste substitute)
- 1 tablespoon coconut aminos
- 1 tablespoon monk fruit sweetener (or stevia)
- 1 teaspoon grated ginger
- 1/2 cup almond flour
- 1 tablespoon coconut aminos
- 1 tablespoon garlic powder
- 1/2 teaspoon salt

For the Korean sauce:
- 1 tablespoon rice vinegar
- 1 tablespoon sesame oil
- 1 clove garlic, minced

Directions:

(1) Turn the oven up to its highest setting (400°F, 200°C). Sprinkle parchment paper on a baking pan. **(2)** Blend together almond flour, garlic powder, paprika, salt, pepper, almond milk, coconut aminos, and olive oil in a big bowl to make batter. **(3)** Mix the batter with the cauliflower florets until they are coated evenly. **(4)** Make a single layer on the baking pan with the oiled cauliflower. Turn once throughout the 20-minute cooking time or until golden. **(5)** In a separate bowl, mix together all the ingredients for the Korean sauce while the dish is baking. **(6)** Take the cauliflower out of the oven, coat it with the Korean sauce, and return it to the oven for another 5 to 7 minutes or until it becomes somewhat crispy. **(7)** While still heated, top with green onions and sesame seeds if you choose.

76. LEMON BUTTER ASPARAGUS

Total Time: 15 minutes | Prep Time: 5 minutes | Cook Time: 10 minutes | Servings: 4

Ingredients:

1 lb (450g) fresh asparagus, trimmed	2 tablespoons grass-fed butter
1 tablespoon olive oil	2 garlic cloves, minced
Juice of 1/2 lemon	Zest of 1 lemon
Salt and pepper, to taste	Optional garnish: grated Parmesan (optional for keto-friendly), fresh parsley

Directions:

(1) Get a big skillet up to medium-high heat. Cut in some butter and olive oil. **(2)** Chop some garlic and sauté it for a minute once the butter has melted. **(3)** Before adding the asparagus, mix them in the garlic butter to coat them. **(4)** Stirring regularly, cook the asparagus for 5-7 minutes or until it reaches a tender-crisp texture. **(5)** Before serving, garnish the asparagus with the zest and squeeze of fresh lemon. **(6)** To taste, season with salt and pepper. **(7)** After taking it off the stove, you may add some Parmesan or parsley as a garnish. Make sure to serve right away.

77. ZUCCHINI GRILLED CHEESE

Total Time: 30 minutes | Prep Time: 15 minutes | Cook Time: 15 minutes | Servings: 2

Ingredients:

2 medium zucchinis, grated	1/2 teaspoon salt
1/4 cup almond flour	1/4 cup grated Parmesan cheese
1 large egg	1/2 teaspoon garlic powder
1/4 teaspoon black pepper	4 slices mozzarella or provolone cheese (or any preferred low-fat cheese)
1 tablespoon olive oil	

Directions:

(1) In a basin, add the shredded zucchini and season with salt. Retain for ten minutes before removing excess moisture with a fresh dishcloth. **(2)** Add the almond flour, zucchini, Parmesan, egg, garlic powder, and black pepper to a big bowl. Bring everything together. Completely combine to create batter consistency. **(3)** Grease a nonstick pan with butter or olive oil and set it over medium heat. **(4)** Transfer about 1/4 cup of the mixture to the pan and press it down into a circular "bread" form that is approximately 1/4 inch thick. Go around the clock four times. **(5)** To get a golden brown and solid finish, cook for 3 to 4 minutes on each side. **(6)** Return to the pan once you've cooked all of the zucchini "bread" slices. In between each circle, put the cheese. **(7)** Cook for an extra two or three minutes on each side to crisp up the outside and melt the cheese. Warm it up and enjoy a low-carb take on grilled cheese!

78. KETO CHEESEBURGER SOUP

Total Time: 30 minutes | Prep Time: 10 minutes | Cook Time: 20 minutes | Servings: 4

Ingredients:

1 lb (450g) ground beef (lean or grass-fed preferred)	1 tablespoon olive oil
1/2 cup onion, diced	1/2 cup celery, diced
2 cloves garlic, minced	2 cups beef broth (low-sodium)
1 cup heavy cream	1/2 cup cream cheese, softened
1 cup shredded cheddar cheese	1 tablespoon mustard (Dijon or yellow)
1 teaspoon paprika	1/4 teaspoon black pepper
Optional toppings: diced pickles, shredded lettuce,	

crumbled bacon, additional cheddar cheese

Directions:

(1) The best way to heat olive oil is in a large pot over medium heat. Brown the ground beef by adding it to the pan. If needed, remove any surplus fat. **(2)** Chop some celery, onion, and garlic and throw them in the saucepan. Allow to cook for around three to four minutes or until the vegetable is well cooked. **(3)** Lower the heat to low and stir in the beef broth. **(4)** Add the melted and smooth cream cheese and stir to combine. **(5)** Cream, cheddar, mustard, paprika, and pepper should be added. Mix thoroughly. **(6)** Simmer the heavy cream for 10 minutes, stirring occasionally, or until it thickens. Reevaluate the seasoning according to your taste. **(7)** For a full-on cheeseburger experience, top with pickles, lettuce, or bacon before serving hot.

79. BROCCOLI CHEDDAR FRITTATA

Total Time: 30 minutes | Prep Time: 10 minutes | Cook Time: 20 minutes | Servings: 4

Ingredients:

1 ½ cups broccoli florets, chopped	6 large eggs
¼ cup unsweetened almond milk (or low-fat milk)	½ cup sharp cheddar cheese, shredded
2 tablespoons green onions, chopped	1 tablespoon olive oil
½ teaspoon garlic powder	¼ teaspoon black pepper
¼ teaspoon sea salt	Cooking spray (optional for greasing the pan)

Directions:

(1) Turn the oven on high heat to 375°F. **(2)** With an oven-safe skillet set over medium heat, warm the olive oil. Chop the broccoli and sauté it for three to four minutes or until it's soft. **(3)** Combine almond milk, eggs, salt, pepper, garlic powder, and a medium bowl; whisk to combine. **(4)** Top the broccoli in the pan with the egg mixture. After that, distribute the green onions and shredded cheddar cheese equally. **(5)** Allow to cook for two or three minutes in a skillet until the edges start to harden. **(6)** To make sure the frittata puffs up and cooks through in the middle, pop it into a preheated oven for 12–15 minutes. Remove the pan from the oven. **(7)** After taking it out of the oven, let it cool for a while before slicing and serving warm.

80. SALMON AND SPINACH OMELET

Total Time: 20 minutes | Prep Time: 10 minutes | Cook Time: 10 minutes | Servings: 2

Ingredients:

4 large eggs	2 tablespoons unsweetened almond milk
½ cup cooked salmon, flaked (leftover or canned works!)	1 cup baby spinach, chopped
1 tablespoon olive oil or avocado oil	¼ teaspoon sea salt
¼ teaspoon black pepper	1 tablespoon fresh dill, chopped (optional)
Lemon wedge for serving (optional)	

Directions:

(1) The eggs, almond milk, salt, and pepper should be whisked together in a basin. **(2)** Warm the olive oil in a pan that does not stick over medium heat. **(3)** The chopped spinach should wilt in a minute or two of cooking, stirring periodically. Make sure the egg mixture spreads out evenly by tilting the pan as you pour it into the pan. For one or two minutes, do not stir it while it cooks. **(4)** As soon as the eggs start to set, divide the omelet in half and top each half with flakes, salmon, and fresh dill. **(5)** Continue cooking for one to two minutes or until the eggs are set but still somewhat soft. **(6)** After flipping the omelet over, carefully transfer it to a serving dish. **(7)** Warm it up and, if you want, serve it with a slice of lemon.

81. PESTO STUFFED CHICKEN BREASTS

Total Time: 40 minutes | Prep Time: 15 minutes | Cook Time: 25 minutes | Servings: 4

Ingredients:

4 boneless, skinless chicken breasts	¼ cup pesto sauce (store-bought or homemade)
½ cup mozzarella cheese, shredded	2 tablespoons sun-dried tomatoes, chopped
1 tablespoon olive oil	½ teaspoon garlic powder
½ teaspoon dried basil	¼ teaspoon sea salt
¼ teaspoon black pepper	Toothpicks (optional)

Directions:

(1) Get your oven preheated to 375°F, which is 190°C. **(2)** Carefully use a sharp knife to carve a tiny pocket into the side of each chicken breast, being careful not to cut through. Combine the sun-dried tomatoes, mozzarella cheese, and pesto in a small bowl. **(3)** Insert a pesto mixture into each chicken breast and, if necessary, use toothpicks to keep them in place. **(4)** Along with salt and pepper, add dried basil and garlic powder to the chicken breasts. A big oven-safe skillet should be heated to a medium temperature with the olive oil. Grill the chicken breasts for three to four minutes on each side or until they become a golden brown color. **(5)** It should take around fifteen to twenty minutes in a preheated oven until the chicken achieves an internal heat of 165 degrees Fahrenheit or 74 degrees Celsius. Remove the pan from the oven. **(6)** After removing the toothpicks, let aside for a few minutes to rest before serving.

82. ROASTED GARLIC PARMESAN BROCCOLI

Total Time: 25 minutes | Prep Time: 10 minutes | Cook Time: 15 minutes | Servings: 4

Ingredients:

4 cups broccoli florets	2 tablespoons olive oil
2 cloves garlic, minced	¼ teaspoon sea salt
¼ teaspoon black pepper	¼ teaspoon red pepper flakes (optional)
¼ cup grated Parmesan cheese	Lemon wedge for serving (optional)

Directions:

(1) Set oven temperature to 400°F. **(2)** Season the broccoli florets with salt, pepper, garlic powder, olive oil, and red pepper flakes (if using) in a big bowl. **(3)** Arrange the broccoli in a uniform fashion on a parchment-lined baking sheet. **(4)** Cook the broccoli for 12–15 minutes or until it becomes soft and the edges become crispy. **(5)** After taking it out of the oven, immediately top it with Parmesan cheese that has been grated. **(6)** If preferred, serve warm and garnish with a squeeze of lemon.

83. GRILLED STEAK SALAD WITH AVOCADO

Total Time: 30 minutes | Prep Time: 15 minutes | Cook Time: 15 minutes | Servings: 2

Ingredients:

8 oz flank steak (or sirloin), trimmed	1 tablespoon olive oil
1 teaspoon garlic powder	1 teaspoon paprika
Salt and pepper to taste	4 cups mixed salad greens
1/2 cup cherry tomatoes, halved	1/4 cup red onion, thinly sliced
1/2 cucumber, sliced	1 avocado, sliced
2 tablespoons crumbled feta cheese (optional)	2 tablespoons balsamic vinaigrette or olive oil and lemon juice

Directions:

(1) Bring a grill pan or outdoor grill up to temperature over medium-high. **(2)** Before seasoning the meat, mix in the olive oil, pepper, garlic powder, and paprika. Cook the steak for four to five minutes on each side of the grill or until done to your liking. After five minutes of resting, thinly slice it against the grain. **(3)** Toss the avocado, cucumber, tomatoes, red onion, and greens in a large salad dish. **(4)** Pile on some sliced steak and, if you're using it, some feta. **(5)** Just before serving, toss with balsamic vinaigrette, olive oil, and lemon juice.

84. THAI PEANUT ZOODLE SALAD

Total Time: 20 minutes | Prep Time: 15 minutes | Cook Time: 5 minutes | Servings: 2

Ingredients:

2 medium zucchinis, spiralized	1/2 red bell pepper, thinly sliced
1/2 cup shredded carrots	1/4 cup chopped cilantro
2 tablespoons roasted peanuts, chopped	1 tablespoon sesame seeds (optional)
1 tablespoon olive oil (optional for sautéing zoodles)	For the Peanut Dressing:
2 tablespoons natural peanut butter	1 tablespoon low-sodium soy sauce
1 tablespoon rice vinegar or lime juice	1 teaspoon sesame oil
1 teaspoon honey (optional, or monk fruit sweetener for lower carbs)	1 small garlic clove, minced
1-2 tablespoons water to thin, as needed	

Directions:

(1) Whisk together the peanut dressing ingredients in a small bowl until well-mixed. If it's too thick to drizzle, add more water. **(2)** Lightly sauté zoodles in olive oil for one or two minutes before removing from heat if you want warm zoodles. If you like a crunchier texture, you may leave them uncooked. **(3)** Throw the zucchini noodles, bell pepper, carrots, cilantro, and a big bowl into a mix. **(4)** Gently cover the salad with the peanut dressing by pouring it over it. **(5)** Chop some peanuts and sesame seeds and sprinkle them on top. Make sure to serve right away.

85. LOW-CARB BEEF AND VEGGIE STIR-FRY

Total Time: 25 minutes | Prep Time: 10 minutes | Cook Time: 15 minutes | Servings: 2

Ingredients:

8 oz lean beef (sirloin or flank steak), thinly sliced	1 tablespoon olive oil or avocado oil
1 cup broccoli florets	1/2 red bell pepper, thinly sliced

1/2 cup sliced mushrooms
2 cloves garlic, minced
2 tablespoons low-sodium soy sauce (or coconut aminos)
1 teaspoon sesame oil
1 teaspoon sesame seeds (optional for garnish)
1/4 cup green onions, chopped
1 tablespoon fresh ginger, grated
1 tablespoon rice vinegar
1/2 teaspoon red pepper flakes (optional)

Directions:

(1) A big skillet or wok set over medium-high heat should be heated with olive oil. **(2)** Saute the beef slices for three to four minutes or until they begin to brown. Take it off the heat and put it aside. **(3)** Toss in a little extra oil if necessary, and sauté the ginger and garlic for 30 seconds or until they release their aroma. **(4)** Combine the mushrooms, bell pepper, broccoli, and onion. To get crisp-tender vegetables, stir-fry for four to five minutes. **(5)** Stir in the rice vinegar, soy sauce, sesame oil, and red pepper flakes before returning the meat to the pan. After you've mixed everything well, cook it for another two minutes. **(6)** Sesame seeds and green onions are good garnishes to add before serving.

86. GREEK YOGURT TZATZIKI SAUCE

Total Time: 10 minutes | Prep Time: 10 minutes | Servings: 6 (about two tablespoons per serving)

Ingredients:

1 cup plain Greek yogurt
2 cloves garlic, minced
1/2 cucumber, peeled, seeded, and finely grated
1 tablespoon olive oil
1 tablespoon fresh lemon juice
Salt and pepper to taste
1 tablespoon fresh dill, chopped (or one teaspoon dried dill)

Directions:

(1) To prevent the cucumber from becoming too soggy, shred it before wrapping it in a clean dish towel or paper towel. Toss together the dill, cucumber, garlic, olive oil, and Greek yogurt in a medium bowl. **(2)** Blend until the blend reaches a velvety consistency. **(3)** To taste, add salt and pepper. **(4)** Allow the flavors to combine by chilling in the fridge for at least 15 minutes. **(5)** Dip, grilled meat sauce, or salad dressing are all good ways to use this.

87. SHRIMP STIR-FRY WITH ZOODLES

Total Time: 20 minutes | Prep Time: 10 minutes | Cook Time: 10 minutes | Servings: 2

Ingredients:

1 lb large shrimp, peeled and deveined
1 tablespoon olive oil
1 red bell pepper, thinly sliced
2 tablespoons low-sodium soy sauce (or coconut aminos)
1 teaspoon fresh ginger, grated
Salt and pepper to taste
2 green onions, sliced (optional, for garnish)
2 medium zucchinis, spiralized
2 cloves garlic, minced
1/2 cup snap peas
1 tablespoon sesame oil
1/4 teaspoon red pepper flakes (optional)
1 tablespoon sesame seeds (optional, for garnish)

Directions:

(1) Spread out the olive oil and set it over medium heat in a large pan. **(2)** After 30 seconds, add the ginger and garlic and cook until they smell good. *(3)* Toss in the shrimp and cook for two to three minutes on each side or until opaque pink and done. Rinse the shrimp and put them aside. *(4)* Throw in some snap peas and red bell peppers in the same pan. Sauté for two to three minutes or until tender-crisp. *(5)* Cook, stirring often, for two more minutes after adding the spiralized zucchini noodles. *(6)* Put the shrimp back in the pan. Include red pepper flakes, sesame oil, and soy sauce. Heat through and mix all ingredients by tossing them together. *(7)* To taste, add salt and pepper. *(8)* Before serving, garnish with green onions & sesame seeds.

88. CREAMY LEMON GARLIC SCALLOPS

Total Time: 25 minutes | Prep Time: 10 minutes | Cook Time: 15 minutes | Servings: 2

Ingredients:

1 lb sea scallops, patted dry	1 tablespoon olive oil
2 tablespoons unsalted butter	3 cloves garlic, minced
Juice and zest of 1 lemon	1/4 cup low-sodium chicken broth
1/4 cup unsweetened coconut cream (or heavy cream if preferred)	2 tablespoons fresh parsley, chopped
Salt and pepper to taste	Lemon slices, for garnish

Directions:

(1) Put some salt and pepper on the scallops and season them on both sides. *(2)* Toss the olive oil into a large pan and heat it over medium-high heat. *(3)* Sear the scallops for two or three minutes on each side or until they turn a golden brown and become opaque in a single layer. Before setting aside, move the scallops to a platter. *(4)* Melt the butter in the same skillet. For a minute, or until aromatic, add garlic and cook. *(5)* Lemon zest, chicken broth, and juice should be stirred in. Simmer for two to three minutes. *(6)* Toss in the coconut cream and turn the heat down to low. The sauce should gradually thicken after simmering for another two or three minutes. *(7)* Put the scallops back in the pan, pour the sauce over them, and heat them for another minute or two. *(8)* Before serving, garnish with chopped parsley and slices of lemon.

89. BLACKENED SALMON WITH AVOCADO SALSA

Total Time: 25 minutes | Prep Time: 10 minutes | Cook Time: 15 minutes | Servings: 2

Ingredients:

For the Salmon:

2 salmon fillets (about 6 oz each)	1 tablespoon olive oil
1 teaspoon smoked paprika	1 teaspoon garlic powder
1/2 teaspoon onion powder	1/2 teaspoon dried thyme
1/2 teaspoon dried oregano	1/4 teaspoon cayenne pepper
Salt and pepper to taste	

For the Avocado Salsa:

1 ripe avocado, diced	1/2 small red onion, finely diced
1/2 cup cherry tomatoes, quartered	2 tablespoons cilantro, chopped
Juice of 1 lime	Salt and pepper to taste

Directions:

(1) A small bowl should be used to whisk the paprika, garlic powder, onion powder, thyme, oregano, cayenne, salt, and pepper. *(2)* Apply

the spice mixture equally to the salmon fillets on both sides. *(3)* The olive oil should be heated in a pan over medium-high heat. 4. *(4)* To get a blackened and cooked-through appearance, grill the salmon fillets for four to five minutes on each side. *(5)* Meanwhile, make a bowl and toss in the avocado, red onion, cherry tomatoes, cilantro, lime juice, salt, and pepper. Gently mix until combined. *(6)* Add some fresh avocado salsa on top of the charred salmon and serve.

90. LEMON HERB ZOODLE SALAD

Total Time: 15 minutes | Prep Time: 15 minutes | Servings: 2

Ingredients:

2 medium zucchinis, spiralized	1/2 cup cherry tomatoes, halved
1/4 cup red onion, thinly sliced	1/4 cup cucumber, sliced
2 tablespoons fresh parsley, chopped	1 tablespoon fresh basil, chopped
2 tablespoons olive oil	Juice and zest of 1 lemon
1 teaspoon Dijon mustard	1 clove garlic, minced
Salt and pepper to taste	1 tablespoon pine nuts or slivered almonds (optional, for garnish)

Directions:

(1) Spaghetti squash, cherry tomatoes, red onion, cucumber, parsley, and basil should all be mixed together in a big basin. *(2)* Combine the olive oil, Garlic, Salt, Pepper, Lemon Zest, Lemon Juice, Dijon Mustard, and Garlic in a mixing bowl. *(3)* Toss the salad in the dressing until it is evenly covered. *(4)* Pine nuts or slivered almonds may be used as a garnish if preferred. *(5)* Feel free to serve it right away or chill it for a chilled alternative by putting it in the fridge for 10-15 minutes.

91. LOW-CARB BEEF AND BROCCOLI

Total Time: 25 minutes | Prep Time: 10 minutes | Cook Time: 15 minutes

Ingredients:

1 lb flank steak	3 cups broccoli florets
2 tbsp avocado oil (or olive oil)	3 cloves garlic, minced
1/4 cup low-sodium soy sauce (or coconut aminos)	1 tbsp oyster sauce (optional for extra flavor)
1 tbsp sesame oil	1 tsp grated fresh ginger
1 tbsp sesame seeds (optional garnish)	2 green onions, sliced (optional garnish)

Directions:

(1) Assemble Your Sauce Blend Chop the ginger into tiny pieces and mix with the sesame oil, soy sauce, and oyster sauce (if using) in a small bowl. Remove off the table. *(2)* Get the Beef Done: While the pan is heated over medium-high heat, add one tablespoon of avocado oil and stir to coat. Lay down a single layer of sliced meat. Cook for two or three minutes on each side in a skillet until golden. Set aside the steak after removing it from the pan. *(3)* Sauté the broccoli with a tablespoon of oil in the same pan. After stirring for a few minutes, add the broccoli florets and cook until they are just crisp-tender. After 30 seconds of stirring, add the minced garlic. *(4)* Mix and Heat: Put the meat back in the pan. Top the broccoli and meat with the sauce. Heat through, stirring occasionally, for another two or three minutes. *(5)* If you choose, you may top it with green onions and sesame seeds before serving. Heat and serve immediately.

92. GRILLED LEMON ASPARAGUS

Total Time: 15 minutes | Prep Time: 5 minutes | Cook Time: 10 minutes

Ingredients:

- 1 lb fresh asparagus, trimmed
- 1 tbsp olive oil
- 1 tbsp lemon juice
- 1 tsp lemon zest
- 1/2 tsp garlic powder
- Salt and black pepper, to taste
- Optional garnish: grated Parmesan cheese or crushed red pepper flakes

Directions:

(1) Grill or pan-saute food over medium-high heat to prepare the grill. **(2)** Place the asparagus in a big basin and coat it well with the olive oil, zest of the lemon, garlic powder, salt, and pepper. Season with lemon juice and pepper. **(3)** Grill: Arrange the asparagus stalks in a single layer on the grill. To get grill marks and tenderness, cook for four to five minutes, flipping once. **(4)** To serve, take it off the grill and place it on a platter. For an optional garnish, you may use Parmesan or red pepper flakes. Make sure to serve right away.

93. GRILLED LEMON CHICKEN KABOBS

Total Time: 30 minutes (plus optional 1-hour marination) | Prep Time: 10 minutes | Cook Time: 15-20 minutes

Ingredients:

- 1.5 lbs boneless, skinless chicken breast pieces
- 2 tbsp olive oil
- 2 tbsp lemon juice
- 1 tbsp lemon zest
- 3 cloves garlic, minced
- 1 tsp dried oregano
- 1/2 tsp paprika
- Salt and black pepper, to taste
- Optional: lemon wedges
- Skewers

Directions:

(1) To marinate the chicken, combine the olive oil, lemon zest and juice, garlic, oregano, paprika, salt, and pepper in a big basin. Whisk to combine. Coat the chicken pieces by adding them and tossing them. Let it marinate for 15 minutes or longer if you want a stronger taste. **(2)** Grill or pan-saute food over medium-high heat to prepare the grill. **(3)** Gather the Kabob Element: Poke holes in the chicken and thread marinated bits onto them. **(4)** Cook the kabobs on a grill for 12–15 minutes, rotating once or twice, or until the chicken is opaque throughout and browned. For best results, aim for a temperature of 165 °F. **(5)** As a finishing touch, top with chopped fresh parsley and pass the lemon wedges separately.

94. SHRIMP SCAMPI WITH ZOODLES

Total Time: 20 minutes | Prep Time: 10 minutes | Cook Time: 10 minutes

Ingredients:

- 1 lb large shrimp, peeled and deveined
- 3 medium zucchini, spiralized into noodles
- 2 tbsp olive oil
- 3 cloves garlic, minced
- 1/4 cup chicken broth
- 2 tbsp lemon juice
- 1/4 tsp red pepper flakes (optional)
- 2 tbsp fresh parsley, chopped
- Salt and black pepper, to taste
- 2 tbsp grated Parmesan cheese (optional)

Directions:

(1) Start by spiralizing the zucchini and setting it aside to make the zoodles. To eliminate any surplus of moisture, gently pat dry using paper towels. *(2)* Toss the shrimp into a large pan and sauté in olive oil that has been heated to medium heat. *(3)* After the garlic starts to release some aroma, toss it into the pan and continue cooking for another 30 seconds. Garnish with shrimp and season with salt, pepper, and red pepper flakes. Sauté for two to three minutes on each side or until opaque and pink. *(4)* Rinse the shrimp and put them aside. *(5)* To prepare the sauce, transfer the chicken stock and lemon juice to the same skillet. Reduce heat to low and simmer for two or three minutes. *(6)* Throw in some Zoodles: Toss some zucchini noodles into the pan and coat them with sauce. Just until softened, cook for two to three minutes. *(7)* Mix well and enjoy! Put the shrimp back in the pan. *(8)* Combine all of the ingredients and, if desired, top with Parmesan and parsley. Heat and serve immediately.

95. BACON-WRAPPED BRUSSELS SPROUTS

Total Time: 30 minutes | Prep Time: 10 minutes | Cook Time: 20 minutes | Servings: 4

Ingredients:

1 lb Brussels sprouts, trimmed and halved	8 slices uncured turkey bacon, halved
1 tbsp olive oil	1 tsp garlic powder
1/2 tsp smoked paprika	1/4 tsp black pepper
Optional: toothpicks for securing	

Directions:

(1) Set the oven temperature to 400°F. Sprinkle parchment paper on a baking pan. *(2)* Arrange the Brussels sprouts in a bowl and coat them evenly with garlic powder, black pepper, smoky paprika, and olive oil. Toss to combine. *(3)* Use half a piece of turkey bacon to wrap each side of a Brussels sprout. If necessary, use a toothpick to secure it. *(4)* On a baking sheet, arrange the Brussels sprouts that have been wrapped, seam side down. *(5)* Cook, turning once, for 20 minutes, or until bacon is crisp and sprouts are soft. *(6)* Take it out of the oven and give it a little time to cool. Enjoy warm for a snack or appetizer.

96. GARLIC BUTTER SHRIMP AND VEGGIES

Total Time: 20 minutes | Prep Time: 10 minutes | Cook Time: 10 minutes | Servings: 4

Ingredients:

1 lb large shrimp, peeled and deveined	2 tbsp unsalted butter (or ghee)
4 cloves garlic, minced	1 small zucchini, sliced
1 red bell pepper, sliced	1 cup broccoli florets
1 tbsp olive oil	1/2 tsp paprika
1/4 tsp red pepper flakes (optional)	Salt and black pepper, to taste
1 tbsp fresh parsley, chopped	1 tbsp lemon juice

Directions:

(1) Spread out the olive oil and set it over medium heat in a large pan. Throw in the broccoli, bell pepper, and zucchini. After 5 or 6 minutes of sautéing, the vegetables should be only slightly softened. Take it out of the pan and put it aside. *(2)* Butter should be melted over medium heat in the same skillet. Saute for 1 minute or until aromatic, adding minced garlic. *(3)* Then, toss in the shrimp. Toss in more paprika, salt, and pepper to taste; for heat, garnish with red pepper flakes. Sauté for two to three minutes on each side or until opaque and pink. *(4)* Throw back the sautéed

vegetables and mix well. Pour some lemon juice over the top and sprinkle some fresh parsley on top. **(5)** It goes well with cauliflower rice or as a standalone dish when served hot.

97. SAUSAGE AND PEPPER BAKE

Total Time: 40 minutes | Prep Time: 10 minutes | Cook Time: 30 minutes | Servings: 4

Ingredients:

4 turkey sausages (nitrate-free), sliced into 1-inch pieces	1 red bell pepper, sliced
1 yellow bell pepper, sliced	1 green bell pepper, sliced
1 small red onion, sliced	2 tbsp olive oil
1 tsp Italian seasoning	1/2 tsp garlic powder
1/4 tsp crushed red pepper flakes	Salt and pepper, to taste
1 tbsp fresh basil or parsley, chopped (optional garnish)	

Directions:

(1) Set the oven temperature to 400°F. To get a baking sheet ready, grease it or line it with parchment paper. **(2)** Sausage, bell pepper, and onion slices should be mixed together in a big basin. Put a little olive oil on top. **(3)** Finish with salt, pepper, garlic powder, crushed red pepper flakes (if desired), and Italian seasoning. Combine all ingredients and stir until covered. **(4)** Once the baking sheet is ready, spread the sausage and pepper mixture evenly over it. **(5)** As the peppers and sausages brown, stir them once midway through the cooking process, which takes 25 to 30 minutes. When done, take it out of the oven and top with chopped fresh herbs. Keep heated before serving.

98. TURKEY SAUSAGE AND EGGPLANT SKILLET

Total Time: 30 minutes | Prep Time: 10 minutes | Cook Time: 20 minutes | Servings: 4

Ingredients:

1 lb turkey sausage (casings removed if using links)	1 medium eggplant, diced
1 small zucchini, diced	1/2 cup cherry tomatoes, halved
2 cloves garlic, minced	2 tbsp olive oil
1/2 tsp dried oregano	1/2 tsp dried basil
Salt and pepper, to taste	2 tbsp grated Parmesan cheese (optional)
1 tbsp fresh parsley, chopped	

Directions:

(1) In a large skillet set over medium-high heat, warm up one tablespoon of olive oil. After approximately five to seven minutes of cooking, add the turkey sausage and continue cooking until it is browned and crumbles easily when pressed with a spatula. **(2)** Before setting aside, move the sausage to a platter. **(3)** Put the last tablespoon of olive oil into the same pan. Toss in the chopped eggplant and cook for about 5 minutes or until it begins to crumble. **(4)** Toss in the zucchini, cherry tomatoes, garlic, oregano, and basil after seasoning with salt and pepper. To get soft veggies, continue cooking for an additional 5 to 7 minutes. **(5)** Put the cooked sausage back in the pan and give it a good swirl. Transfer to a skillet and cook for two or three minutes or until well heated. **(6)** If you want, you may top it up with a little Parmesan and fresh parsley. Hot is best.

99. GRILLED PORTOBELLO MUSHROOM BURGERS

Total Time: 25 minutes | Prep Time: 10 minutes

Ingredients:

4 large Portobello mushrooms	2 tbsp olive oil
1 tbsp balsamic vinegar	1 tsp garlic powder
1/2 tsp salt	1/2 tsp black pepper
4 lettuce leaves (for buns)	1 tomato, sliced
1/2 avocado, sliced	1/4 cup red onion, sliced

Directions:

(1) Grill until it is medium-hot. *(2)* After removing the stems from the Portobello mushrooms, cover them with a combination of olive oil and balsamic vinegar. Toss in some garlic powder and season with salt and pepper. *(3)* To make mushrooms tender, grill them for about 5 minutes on each side. *(4)* Top grilled mushrooms with avocado, red onion, tomato, and lettuce leaves. *(5)* This low-carb burger option is ready to be served right away.

100. HERB-CRUSTED GRILLED TUNA

Total Time: 20 minutes | Prep Time: 5 minutes

Ingredients:

2 tuna steaks (6 oz each)	1 tbsp olive oil
1 tsp Dijon mustard	1 tbsp fresh parsley, chopped
1 tsp fresh thyme, chopped	1/2 tsp garlic powder
1/2 tsp salt	1/2 tsp black pepper

Directions:

(1) Warm up the grill to a medium-high temperature. *(2)* Olive oil and Dijon mustard should be brushed across tuna steaks. *(3)* Toss in the thyme, parsley, garlic powder, and a small bowl after seasoning with black pepper and salt. Distribute the herb mixture evenly over the tuna steaks. *(4)* To achieve medium-rare doneness, grill for two to three minutes on each side or until done to your liking. *(5)* Accompany it promptly with a serving of roasted veggies or leafy greens.

101. AVOCADO EGG SALAD CUPS

Total Time: 15 minutes | Prep Time: 10 minutes

Ingredients:

2 ripe avocados, halved and pitted	4 hard-boiled eggs, chopped
2 tbsp Greek yogurt	1 tsp Dijon mustard
1/2 tsp garlic powder	1/2 tsp salt
1/2 tsp black pepper	1 tbsp fresh chives, chopped

Directions:

(1) Separate the avocados and mash one in a dish. Cut the other into tiny chunks. *(2)* Blend in the Greek yogurt, hard-boiled eggs, Dijon mustard, garlic powder, salt, and pepper. Thoroughly blend. *(3)* Fill the avocado halves with the mixture using a spoon. *(4)* Serve right away with a garnish of fresh chives.

102. LOW-CARB MUSHROOM RISOTTO

Total Time: 30 minutes | Prep Time: 10 minutes

Ingredients:

2 tbsp olive oil	1 small onion, diced
2 cloves garlic, minced	2 cups cauliflower rice
1 cup mushrooms, sliced	1/2 cup unsweetened almond milk
1/4 cup grated Parmesan cheese	1/2 tsp salt
1/2 tsp black pepper	1 tbsp fresh parsley, chopped

Directions:

(1) To get the best results, warm the olive oil in a skillet over medium heat. Get the garlic and onion soft by sautéing them. After 5 minutes of stirring, the mushrooms should be soft. *(2)* Include almond milk, salt, black pepper, cauliflower rice, and cauliflower. Sauté for a further five minutes. *(3)* Add the Parmesan and continue cooking for another two or three minutes or until it becomes creamy. *(4)* Warm and top with fresh parsley.

103. THAI COCONUT CHICKEN SOUP

Total Time: 30 minutes | Prep Time: 10 minutes

Ingredients:

1 lb chicken breast, sliced	1 can (13.5 oz) coconut milk
2 cups chicken broth	1 tbsp coconut oil
1 tbsp red curry paste	1 cup mushrooms, sliced
1 red bell pepper, sliced	1 tbsp fish sauce
1 tbsp lime juice	1-inch ginger, grated
2 cloves garlic, minced	2 green onions, chopped
Fresh cilantro for garnish	

Directions:

(1) Melt the coconut oil in a pot set over medium heat. After one minute of sautéing, add ginger and garlic. *(2)* Cook for a further minute after stirring in the red curry paste. *(3)* Turn the heat down to low and stir in the coconut milk and chicken broth. Toss in some bell peppers, mushrooms, and sliced chicken. Gently cook the chicken for 10 minutes or until done. *(4)* Add the lime juice, green onions, and fish sauce and stir to combine. Allow to simmer for a further two minutes. *(5)* Warm the dish and top it with chopped cilantro.

104. CABBAGE STIR-FRY WITH GROUND BEEF

Total Time: 25 minutes | Prep Time: 10 minutes

Ingredients:

1 lb ground beef	4 cups cabbage, shredded
1 tbsp olive oil	1 small onion, chopped
2 cloves garlic, minced	1 tbsp soy sauce (or coconut aminos)
1 tsp ginger, grated	1/2 tsp red pepper flakes (optional)
1 tbsp apple cider vinegar	

Directions:

(1) Put a little oil in a skillet and place it on medium heat. Gently sauté the garlic and onion in a pan until they soften. Brown the ground beef by adding it to the pan. *(2)* Coat the cabbage with the soy sauce, then add the ginger and red pepper flakes. Until the cabbage is soft, about 7 to 10 minutes. *(3)* After that, whisk in the apple cider vinegar. *(4)* As an entree or a side, serve hot.

105. GRILLED CHICKEN CAESAR SALAD

Total Time: 20 minutes | Prep Time: 10 minutes

Ingredients:

2 boneless, skinless chicken breasts	1 tbsp olive oil
1 tsp garlic powder	6 cups romaine lettuce, chopped
1/4 cup Parmesan cheese, grated	1/2 cup Caesar dressing (keto-friendly)
1/2 avocado, sliced	1 tbsp lemon juice
Salt and pepper to taste	

Directions:

(1) Warm up the grill to a medium-high temperature. **(2)** Aside from salt, pepper, and garlic powder, drizzle olive oil over the chicken. Cook until done. Cook, turning once, for about 7 to 10 minutes on each side. **(3)** Slice the chicken once it has rested for a few minutes. **(4)** Combine the lettuce and Caesar dressing in a big basin and mix well. **(5)** Arrange sliced chicken, avocado, and Parmesan cheese on top. Add a squeeze of lemon juice. **(6)** Make sure to serve right away.

106. AVOCADO EGG BREAKFAST CUPS

Total Time: 20 minutes | Prep Time: 5 minutes

Ingredients:

2 large avocados, halved and pitted	4 eggs
1/4 tsp salt	1/4 tsp black pepper
1/4 tsp paprika	2 tbsp shredded cheese (optional)
2 tbsp cooked bacon bits (optional)	Fresh parsley for garnish

Directions:

(1) Get your oven preheated to 375°F, which is 190°C. **(2)** Remove a little bit of avocado flesh to make room for the eggs. **(3)** To maintain their upright position, place the avocado halves in a baking dish. **(4)** In each avocado half, crack one egg. Add paprika, salt, and pepper. **(5)** To get a set in the egg whites and a soft yolk, bake for 12–15 minutes. Add bacon pieces, cheese, and parsley on top. Keep heated before serving.

107. LEMON GARLIC CHICKEN STIR-FRY

Total Time: 25 minutes | Prep Time: 10 minutes

Ingredients:

2 boneless, skinless chicken breasts	2 tbsp olive oil
3 cloves garlic, minced	1 lemon (juice and zest)
1 cup broccoli florets	

Directions:

(1) Simmer one tablespoon of olive oil in a skillet set over medium heat. Cook the chicken for 5 minutes after adding it. **(2)** After 2 minutes, add the minced garlic and keep cooking. **(3)** Once the broccoli is soft, stir it in and continue cooking for five more minutes. **(4)** Toss the stir-fry well after adding the lemon juice and zest. **(5)** Enjoy while hot!

108. SESAME CAULIFLOWER BITES

Total Time: 30 minutes | Prep Time: 10 minutes

Ingredients:

1 small head of	2 tbsp olive oil

cauliflower
2 tbsp soy sauce
1 tbsp sesame seeds
1 tsp garlic powder

Directions:

(1) Set oven temperature to 400°F. Sprinkle parchment paper on a baking pan. **(2)** Combine the cauliflower with sesame seeds, garlic powder, olive oil, and soy sauce. **(3)** Put it in the oven and bake for 20 minutes, stirring once. Take it out of the oven and let it cool for a little. **(4)** Appetizer or side dish option.

109. LOW-CARB EGGPLANT LASAGNA

Total Time: 40 minutes | Prep Time: 15 minutes

Ingredients:

1 large eggplant, sliced lengthwise	1 cup ricotta cheese
1 cup marinara sauce (low-carb)	1/2 cup shredded mozzarella cheese
1 tsp Italian seasoning	

Directions:

(1) Get your oven preheated to 375°F, which is 190°C. **(2)** After 10 minutes of sitting in a little salt, pat dry the eggplant slices. **(3)** Combine the sliced eggplant, ricotta, marinara sauce, and mozzarella in a baking dish. Put on more layers. **(4)** After 25 minutes in the oven, sprinkle with Italian spice. **(5)** Allow it to cool for a moment before you eat.

110. CAPRESE STUFFED PORTOBELLO MUSHROOMS

Total Time: 20 minutes | Prep Time: 10 minutes

Ingredients:

4 large portobello mushrooms, stems removed	1 cup cherry tomatoes, halved
4 oz fresh mozzarella, sliced	2 tbsp balsamic vinegar
1 tbsp olive oil	

Directions:

(1) Get your oven preheated to 375°F, which is 190°C. **(2)** Before placing the mushrooms on a baking pan, brush them with olive oil. **(3)** Spoon sliced mozzarella and cherry tomatoes into each mushroom. **(4)** Before baking for 15 minutes, drizzle with balsamic vinegar. **(5)** Warm it up and savor it!

111. LOW-CARB BEEF STROGANOFF

Total Time: 30 minutes | Prep Time: 10 minutes

Ingredients:

1 lb beef sirloin, thinly sliced	1 cup mushrooms, sliced
½ cup onion, diced	1 cup heavy cream
2 tbsp butter	

Directions:

(1) While the pan is heated over medium heat, melt the butter. Toss in the mushrooms and onions and cook until they soften. **(2)** Brown the beef slices by adding them to the pan. **(3)** Simmer, whisking constantly, for five minutes or until the heavy cream has thickened. **(4)** To taste, season with salt and pepper. **(5)** Spoon into noodles made with zucchini or rice cooked in cauliflower.

112. BUFFALO CHICKEN ZUCCHINI BOATS

Total Time: 35 minutes | Prep Time: 10 minutes

Ingredients:

- 2 large zucchini, halved lengthwise
- ¼ cup buffalo sauce
- 2 tbsp ranch dressing
- 1 cup shredded cooked chicken
- ½ cup shredded cheddar cheese

Directions:

(1) Get your oven preheated to 375°F, which is 190°C. *(2)* Cut the zucchini in half lengthwise and remove the core. *(3)* Combine the buffalo sauce and shredded chicken in a mixing basin. *(4)* Spoon the chicken mixture into each half of the zucchini and sprinkle with cheese. *(5)* Before serving, bake for 20 to 25 minutes and top with ranch dressing.

113. TERIYAKI ZOODLE BOWLS

Total Time: 25 minutes | Prep Time: 10 minutes

Ingredients:

- 2 medium zucchini, spiralized
- ¼ cup soy sauce (or coconut aminos)
- 1 tbsp sesame seeds
- 1 cup cooked chicken breast, sliced
- 1 tbsp sesame oil

Directions:

(1) In a skillet, warm the sesame oil over medium heat. *(2)* Cook, stirring occasionally, for three to four minutes to reheat the chicken. *(3)* After 2 minutes of simmering, stir in the soy sauce. *(4)* Cook for a further 2 minutes, then add the zoodles and toss to combine. *(5)* Before serving, top with sesame seeds.

114. CREAMY CAULIFLOWER MAC AND CHEESE

Total Time: 30 minutes | Prep Time: 10 minutes

Ingredients:

- 1 head cauliflower, cut into florets
- ½ cup heavy cream
- ¼ tsp garlic powder
- 1 cup shredded cheddar cheese
- 1 tbsp butter

Directions:

(1) After around 10 minutes of steaming, the cauliflower florets should be soft. *(2)* While the butter is melting in a skillet, whisk the heavy cream into it. While cooking, mix in the garlic powder and cheese until smooth. *(3)* Coat the cauliflower evenly with the sauce. *(4)* To make a mac and cheese substitute that is suitable for ketosis, serve warm.

115. BEEF AND MUSHROOM STIR-FRY

Total Time: 25 minutes | Prep Time: 10 minutes

Ingredients:

- 1 lb beef sirloin, thinly sliced
- 2 tbsp coconut aminos (or low-sodium soy sauce)
- 2 cloves garlic, minced
- 2 cups mushrooms, sliced
- 1 tbsp olive oil

Directions:

(1) The olive oil should be heated in a pan over medium-high heat. 4. *(2)* After three or four minutes, brown the meat slices. Take off the heat. *(3)* Cook, stirring occasionally, for three to five minutes or until the garlic and

mushrooms are tender. Put the coconut aminos on top of the steak and put it back in the pan. Add another 2 minutes of stirring. **(4)** Enjoy while hot!

116. ZUCCHINI NOODLES WITH LEMON GARLIC SHRIMP

Total Time: 20 minutes | Prep Time: 10 minutes

Ingredients:

- 2 medium zucchinis, spiralized
- 2 tbsp olive oil
- 1 tbsp lemon juice
- 1/2 lb shrimp, peeled and deveined
- 2 cloves garlic, minced

Directions:

(1) One tablespoon of olive oil may be warmed in a pan and placed over medium heat. Sauté the shrimp for two or three minutes on each side. Take off the heat. **(2)** Put the garlic and the rest of the olive oil into the same pan. After one minute, sauté. **(3)** After two or three minutes, when the noodles are just slightly soft, add the zucchini. **(4)** Put the shrimp back in the pan and add the lemon juice. Mix by tossing. **(5)** Make sure to serve right away.

117. GARLIC BUTTER ROASTED MUSHROOMS

Total Time: 30 minutes | Prep Time: 10 minutes

Ingredients:

- 2 cups whole mushrooms
- 2 cloves garlic, minced
- Salt and pepper to taste
- 2 tbsp butter, melted
- 1 tbsp fresh parsley, chopped

Directions:

(1) Set oven temperature to 400°F. **(2)** Combine the sliced mushrooms with the salted and peppered garlic, melted butter, and a bowl. **(3)** Ensure that the mushrooms are evenly distributed over a baking sheet. **(4)** Turn the roaster halfway through the 20-minute cooking time. **(5)** Top with fresh parsley and enjoy while still warm.

118. TURKEY SAUSAGE BREAKFAST BOWL

Total Time: 20 minutes | Prep Time: 10 minutes

Ingredients:

- 2 turkey sausage links, sliced
- 2 eggs
- 1/2 avocado, sliced
- 2 cups spinach
- 1 tbsp olive oil

Directions:

(1) Put a little oil in a skillet and place it on medium heat. For 5-7 minutes, or until browned, cook the turkey sausage. **(2)** Set aside the sausage and heat the spinach until it wilts. **(3)** Saute the eggs, sunny side up, in a separate pan. **(4)** Sausage, spinach, and eggs should be mixed together in a basin. Top with slices of avocado. **(5)** Warm it up and savor it!

119. SPINACH ARTICHOKE DIP

Total Time: 25 minutes | Prep Time: 10 minutes

Ingredients:

- 1 cup fresh spinach, chopped
- 1/2 cup cream
- 1/2 cup canned artichoke hearts, chopped
- 1/4 cup Greek yogurt

cheese, softened
1/4 cup grated Parmesan cheese
1/2 tsp garlic powder

Directions:

(1) Get your oven preheated to 375°F, which is 190°C. **(2)** Combine the Greek yogurt, garlic powder, and cream cheese in a bowl & stir until combined. **(3)** Add artichokes, spinach, and Parmesan cheese; stir to combine. **(4)** Place in the oven and cook for 15 minutes or until the mixture begins to bubble. **(5)** Warm it up and top it with fresh veggies or low-carb crackers.

120. BAKED GARLIC PARMESAN ZUCCHINI

Total Time: 20 minutes | Prep Time: 5 minutes

Ingredients:

2 medium zucchinis, sliced into rounds
1/4 cup grated Parmesan cheese
1/2 tsp Italian seasoning
2 tbsp olive oil
1/2 tsp garlic powder

Directions:

(1) Set oven temperature to 400°F. **(2)** Combine the sliced zucchini with the Italian seasoning, garlic powder, and olive oil. **(3)** Put them one layer deep on a baking pan. **(4)** Before baking for 12–15 minutes, or until golden, top with Parmesan cheese. **(5)** As a starter or a side dish, serve warm.

121. LOW-CARB CHEESEBURGER CASSEROLE

Total Time: 35 minutes | Prep Time: 10 minutes

Ingredients:

1 lb ground beef
1/2 cup shredded cheddar cheese
2 eggs, beaten
1/2 cup diced onion
1/2 cup heavy cream
1/2 tsp salt & pepper

Directions:

(1) Get your oven preheated to 375°F, which is 190°C. **(2)** Brown the ground beef and onions in a pan over medium heat. **(3)** After any excess fat has been drained, transfer the meat mixture to a baking dish. Combine eggs, heavy cream, pepper, and salt in a mixing bowl. Top with the meat. **(4)** Before baking for 20 minutes, sprinkle cheese on top.

122. PESTO CAULIFLOWER MASH

Total Time: 15 minutes | Prep Time: 5 minutes

Ingredients:

2 cups cauliflower florets
2 tbsp unsalted butter
1/2 tsp salt
2 tbsp pesto sauce
1/4 cup grated Parmesan cheese

Directions:

(1) In order to make cauliflower tender, steam it for around 10 minutes or boil it. **(2)** Place in a food processor after draining. **(3)** Toss in the pesto, mozzarella, salt, and butter. Mix until combined. **(4)** Mash to your preferred flavor. **(5)** Substitute with regular mashed potatoes for a low-carb option.

123. CREAMY COCONUT CURRY SHRIMP

Total Time: 25 minutes | Prep Time: 10 minutes

Ingredients:

1 lb shrimp, peeled and deveined	1 can (13.5 oz) coconut milk
1 tbsp coconut oil	2 cloves garlic, minced
1 tbsp curry powder	

Directions:

(1) Melt the coconut oil in a pot set over medium heat. *(2)* To release its aroma, sauté the garlic for 1 minute. *(3)* Toss in the shrimp and cook for another two or three minutes or until bright pink. *(4)* Stir in the curry powder with the coconut milk. Let it simmer for ten minutes. *(5)* Top with cauliflower rice and serve hot, or eat plain.

124. KETO CHOCOLATE AVOCADO MOUSSE

Total Time: 10 minutes | Prep Time: 5 minutes

Ingredients:

2 ripe avocados	¼ cup unsweetened cocoa powder
¼ cup unsweetened almond milk	2 tbsp keto-friendly sweetener (like monk fruit)
1 tsp vanilla extract	

Directions:

(1) Remove the avocado pit and add the flesh to a blender. *(2)* Blend in the almond milk, cocoa powder, sweetener, and vanilla extract. *(3)* Whisk or mix until combined. *(4)* Put it in the fridge for five minutes to chill before you serve it. *(5)* If desired, top with nuts or keto-friendly whipped cream.

125. CAULIFLOWER GRATIN

Total Time: 40 minutes | Prep Time: 10 minutes

Ingredients:

1 head cauliflower, cut into florets	1 cup heavy cream
1 cup shredded cheddar cheese	¼ cup grated Parmesan cheese
½ tsp garlic powder	

Directions:

(1) Get your oven preheated to 375°F, which is 190°C. *(2)* Soften the cauliflower florets by steaming them for about 5 minutes. *(3)* The ingredients for the cheese sauce include garlic powder, heavy cream, cheddar, and Parmesan. *(4)* After you've tossed the cauliflower in the cheese mixture, transfer it to a baking tray. *(5)* To get a golden brown and bubbly top, bake for 25 minutes.

126. SPINACH ARTICHOKE CHICKEN CASSEROLE

Total Time: 45 minutes | Prep Time: 15 minutes

Ingredients:

2 cups cooked, shredded chicken	1 cup fresh spinach, chopped
1 cup canned artichoke hearts, chopped	1 cup cream cheese, softened
½ cup shredded mozzarella cheese	

Directions:

(1) Get your oven preheated to 375°F, which is 190°C. *(2)* The chicken, spinach, artichokes, cream cheese, and half of the mozzarella should be combined in a bowl. *(3)* Place in a casserole dish that has been buttered and sprinkle the remaining mozzarella on top. *(4)* The cheese should melt and bubble after 30 minutes in the oven. *(5)* Warm it up and savor it!

127. LOW-CARB SHRIMP PAD THAI

Total Time: 25 minutes | Prep Time: 10 minutes

Ingredients:

1 lb shrimp, peeled and deveined	2 cups zucchini noodles (zoodles)
2 eggs, beaten	2 tbsp coconut aminos
1 tbsp olive oil	1 tsp minced garlic

Directions:

(1) Coat the shrimp with olive oil and sear them for a few minutes on each side in a skillet set over medium heat. Detach and put aside. *(2)* In the same skillet, cook the eggs until they are almost set. Toss in the coconut aminos, zucchini noodles, garlic, and oil. Sauté for a further two minutes. *(3)* Put the shrimp back in the pan and mix everything well. *(4)* Garnish with lime wedges or fresh herbs, and serve hot.

128. CREAMY CAULIFLOWER SOUP

Total Time: 30 minutes | Prep Time: 10 minutes

Ingredients:

1 head cauliflower, chopped	3 cups vegetable broth
1 cup unsweetened almond milk	2 tbsp butter
1 tsp garlic powder	Salt and pepper to taste

Directions:

(1) The butter should melt in a pan set over medium heat. Cook the cauliflower for 5 minutes after adding it. *(2)* Toss in the vegetable stock and bring to a boil. Simmer for 15 minutes with the lid on over low heat. *(3)* If using almond milk, add garlic powder, salt, and pepper after blending the soup until smooth. *(4)* Keep it low for another five minutes. *(5)* Warm it up and top it with fresh herbs if you want.

129. GARLIC BUTTER BROCCOLI CASSEROLE

Total Time: 35 minutes | Prep Time: 10 minutes

Ingredients:

4 cups broccoli florets	1 cup shredded cheddar cheese
2 tbsp butter	1 tsp minced garlic
½ cup heavy cream	Salt and pepper to taste

Directions:

(1) Get your oven preheated to 375°F, which is 190°C. *(2)* Just before they are ready to be eaten, steam broccoli for about 5 minutes. *(3)* Melt the butter and sauté the garlic for one minute in a saucepan. When the cheese has melted, whisk in the heavy cream. *(4)* Put the broccoli in a baking dish after mixing it with the sauce. *(5)* To get a golden crust and bubbling center, bake for 20 minutes. Keep heated before serving.

130. GRILLED CHICKEN AND VEGGIE SKEWERS

Total Time: 30 minutes | Prep Time: 10 minutes

Ingredients:

2 chicken breasts, cut into chunks	1 zucchini, sliced
1 bell pepper, cut into chunks	1 tbsp olive oil
1 tsp Italian seasoning	Salt and pepper to

taste

Directions:

(1) Warm up the grill to a medium-high temperature. (2) Pour olive oil, Italian seasoning, salt, and pepper into a bowl; add the chicken and vegetables and mix to coat. (3) Skewer the chicken and veggies in alternate threads. (4) The chicken should be grilled for four to five minutes on each side for full doneness. (5) If you'd like a low-carb dipping sauce on the side, serve it hot.

131. SHRIMP AVOCADO LETTUCE WRAPS

Total Time: 15 minutes | Prep Time: 10 minutes | Cook Time: 5 minutes

Ingredients:

- 1/2 lb cooked shrimp, peeled
- 1 tbsp lime juice
- 6 large lettuce leaves (romaine or butter lettuce)
- 1 avocado, diced
- 1/4 cup red onion, finely chopped

Directions:

(1) Combine the red onion, lime juice, avocado, and shrimp in a bowl. (2) Be careful not to break up the avocado while gently mixing. (3) Scoop up a spoonful of the mixture and distribute it among the lettuce leaves. To make a taco, wrap the lettuce around the filling. (4) Quickly prepare and enjoy!

132. GARLIC BUTTER MUSHROOMS AND SPINACH

Total Time: 15 minutes | Prep Time: 5 minutes | Cook Time: 10 minutes

Ingredients:

- 2 cups mushrooms, sliced
- 2 tbsp butter
- 1/2 tsp salt
- 2 cups fresh spinach
- 2 cloves garlic, minced

Directions:

(1) Put the butter in a pot and melt it over medium heat. After the garlic starts to release some aroma, toss it into the pan and continue cooking for another 30 seconds. (2) If you want soft mushrooms, toss them in and simmer for five to seven minutes. (3) After 2 minutes of stirring, the spinach should have wilted. (4) Add salt, stir to combine, and serve hot.

133. CAULIFLOWER CRUST MARGHERITA PIZZA

Total Time: 40 minutes | Prep Time: 15 minutes | Cook Time: 25 minutes

Ingredients:

- 2 cups cauliflower rice
- 1 egg, beaten
- 1/4 cup tomato sauce
- 5 fresh basil leaves
- 1/2 cup shredded mozzarella cheese
- 1/2 tsp Italian seasoning
- 1/2 cup fresh mozzarella, sliced

Directions:

(1) Set oven temperature to 400°F. (2) Cook the rice with the cauliflower in the microwave for 5 minutes, then use a cloth to press out any extra water. (3) Toss the shredded mozzarella, egg, cauliflower, and spice together in a bowl. (4) Roll out the dough into a crust and place it on a baking pan. Do not remove from oven until 15 minutes have passed. (5) Toss on some basil, fresh

mozzarella, and tomato sauce. Cook for a further ten minutes. Keep heated before serving.

134. CAJUN GRILLED SHRIMP SKEWERS

Total Time: 20 minutes | Prep Time: 10 minutes | Cook Time: 10 minutes

Ingredients:

- 1 lb shrimp, peeled and deveined
- 1 tbsp Cajun seasoning
- 6 wooden skewers (soaked in water)
- 1 tbsp olive oil
- 1/2 tsp garlic powder

Directions:

(1) Warm up the grill to a medium-high temperature. *(2)* Combine the shrimp, garlic powder, Cajun spice, and olive oil in a mixing bowl. *(3)* Embellish skewers with shrimp. *(4)* Sauté for two or three minutes on each side or until no longer pink and fully done. *(5)* Hot, garnish with a squeezed lemon.

135. CAULIFLOWER HASH BROWNS

Total Time: 25 minutes | Prep Time: 10 minutes

Ingredients:

- 2 cups riced cauliflower
- ¼ cup almond flour
- Salt and pepper to taste
- 1 egg, beaten
- ¼ teaspoon garlic powder

Directions:

(1) Get a nonstick skillet hot in a medium saucepan. *(2)* Cauliflower rice, egg, almond flour, garlic powder, salt, and pepper should all be combined in a container. *(3)* Pat the mixture into small patties and add them to the pan. *(4)* To get a golden brown and crispy finish, cook for 3 to 4 minutes on each side. *(5)* Warm it up and savor it!

136. ZOODLE CAPRESE SALAD

Total Time: 15 minutes | Prep Time: 10 minutes

Ingredients:

- 2 medium zucchinis, spiralized
- ¼ cup fresh mozzarella balls
- 1 tablespoon balsamic vinegar
- ½ cup cherry tomatoes, halved
- 1 tablespoon olive oil

Directions:

(1) Mix together the mozzarella balls, spiralized zucchini, and cherry tomatoes in a big basin. *(2)* Toss with olive oil and balsamic vinegar. *(3)* Coat evenly by lightly tossing. *(4)* If you want, you may add salt and pepper. *(5)* Quickly serve as a revitalizing salad.

137. LEMON BUTTER COD WITH SPINACH

Total Time: 20 minutes | Prep Time: 5 minutes

Ingredients:

- 2 cod fillets
- 1 tablespoon lemon juice
- Salt and pepper to taste
- 2 tablespoons butter
- 2 cups fresh spinach

Directions:

(1) Using a medium-sized pan, melt one tablespoon of butter. Cook the fish fillets for three to four minutes on each side after

seasoning them with salt and pepper. **(2)** After removing the fish, return it to the pan with the leftover butter and lemon juice. **(3)** After 2 minutes of sautéing in the sauce, the spinach should have wilted. **(4)** Top spinach with fish and top with lemon butter sauce.

138. CREAMY SPINACH AND MUSHROOM SOUP

Total Time: 30 minutes | Prep Time: 10 minutes

Ingredients:

1 tablespoon olive oil	1 cup mushrooms, sliced
2 cups fresh spinach	2 cups vegetable broth
½ cup unsweetened coconut milk	

Directions:

(1) Put the olive oil in a pot and place it over medium heat. **(2)** After 5 minutes of sautéing, the mushrooms should be tender. **(3)** Simmer after adding vegetable broth. **(4)** After five more minutes, add the spinach and coconut milk and continue cooking. **(5)** For a creamier consistency, blend until smooth. Serve while warm.

139. TERIYAKI CHICKEN STIR-FRY

Total Time: 30 minutes | Prep Time: 10 minutes

Ingredients:

2 boneless, skinless chicken breasts, thinly sliced	1 tablespoon olive oil
1 red bell pepper, sliced	1 green bell pepper, sliced
1 small broccoli crown, cut into florets	1 medium carrot, julienned
1/2 cup snap peas	1/4 cup low-sodium soy sauce
1 tablespoon honey (or sugar-free substitute)	1 teaspoon grated ginger
1 teaspoon minced garlic	1 teaspoon cornstarch mixed with
1/2 teaspoon sesame oil	Sesame seeds and green onions for garnish

Directions:

(1) Toss the olive oil into a large pan and heat it over medium-high heat. After 5 or 6 minutes, add the chicken pieces and brown them. Take it off the heat and put it aside. **(2)** Stir in the snap peas, carrot, bell peppers, broccoli, and skillet. While stirring, cook for three to four minutes or until just starting to get soft. **(3)** Get a small basin and mix together the sesame oil, ginger, garlic, cornstarch slurry, honey, and soy sauce. Add the chicken back to the pan and stir-fry with the sauce. The sauce should thicken after another three to four minutes of cooking after a good tossing. **(4)** Add green onions and sesame seeds as garnishes. Heat and serve immediately.

140. EGGPLANT PARMESAN STACKS

Total Time: 40 minutes | Prep Time: 15 minutes

Ingredients:

1 large eggplant	1 cup almond flour
1 teaspoon garlic powder	1 teaspoon Italian seasoning
1/2 teaspoon salt	1/2 teaspoon black pepper
1 egg, beaten	1 cup sugar-free marinara sauce
1/2 cup shredded	1/4 cup grated

mozzarella cheese	Parmesan cheese
1 tablespoon olive oil	Fresh basil leaves for garnish

Directions:

(1) Get your oven preheated to 375°F, which is 190°C. Sprinkle parchment paper on a baking pan. **(2)** In a basin, mix together almond flour, garlic powder, Italian seasoning, salt, and black pepper. **(3)** Coat each slice of eggplant with the almond flour mixture after dipping it into the beaten egg. **(4)** Grill the eggplant slices in a pan coated with olive oil for 2 minutes on each side, or until they become a golden color, over medium heat. Move the mixture to the baking pan. **(5)** Distribute mozzarella, Parmesan, and marinara sauce over the eggplant slices. **(6)** Bake the cheese for about 15 minutes or until it melts and bubbles. **(7)** Serve heated with a sprinkle of fresh basil.

141. GRILLED LEMON HERB CHICKEN BREASTS

Total Time: 25 minutes | Prep Time: 10 minutes

Ingredients:

2 boneless, skinless chicken breasts	2 tablespoons olive oil
2 tablespoons lemon juice	1 teaspoon lemon zest
1 teaspoon dried oregano	1 teaspoon garlic powder
1/2 teaspoon salt	1/2 teaspoon black pepper
1/4 teaspoon red pepper flakes (optional)	Fresh parsley for garnish

Directions:

(1) Whisk together the garlic powder, lemon zest and juice, oregano, olive oil, salt, pepper, and red pepper flakes in a small bowl. Season with salt and pepper to taste. Mix in the salt and pepper. **(2)** To enhance the taste, marinate the chicken breasts for a minimum of 10 minutes and a maximum of an hour. Coat them with the marinade. **(3)** Bring a grill pan or grill out to medium heat. **(4)** To ensure doneness, grill the chicken for 5 to 7 minutes on each side or until the internal temperature reaches 165°F. **(5)** Add fresh parsley as a garnish after it has rested for a few minutes. Pair with a side salad & roasted veggies for a delicious meal.

142. BUFFALO CAULIFLOWER WINGS

Total Time: 35 minutes | Prep Time: 10 minutes

Ingredients:

1 medium head of cauliflower	1/2 cup almond flour
1/2 teaspoon garlic powder	1/2 teaspoon onion powder
1/2 teaspoon smoked paprika	1/2 teaspoon salt
1/4 teaspoon black pepper	1/2 cup unsweetened almond milk
1/2 cup sugar-free buffalo sauce	1 tablespoon melted butter (or dairy-free alternative)
1 teaspoon apple cider vinegar	Chopped green onions for garnish

Directions:

(1) Set oven temperature to 400°F. Sprinkle parchment paper on a baking pan. **(2)** In a bowl, combine onion and garlic powders, almond flour, smoked paprika, salt, and pepper. Shake to combine. **(3)** After dipping the cauliflower florets in almond milk, coat them with the flour mixture. Bake the florets for 20 minutes after arranging them on the baking pan. **(4)** Whisk together the buffalo sauce, apple cider vinegar, and melted butter in a small bowl while the dish is in the oven.

(5) After 10 or 12 more minutes in the oven, take the cauliflower out and toss it with the buffalo sauce. **(6)** Serve with a nutritious dipping sauce and top with chopped green onions.

143. ROASTED RADISH AND ZUCCHINI

Total Time: 30 minutes | Prep Time: 10 minutes

Ingredients:

1 cup radishes, halved	1 zucchini, sliced into rounds
1 tbsp olive oil	½ tsp garlic powder
½ tsp paprika	½ tsp salt
¼ tsp black pepper	1 tsp lemon juice
1 tbsp fresh parsley, chopped	

Directions:

(1) Set oven temperature to 400°F. **(2)** Combine radishes and zucchini in a bowl and add olive oil, garlic powder, paprika, salt, and pepper. Toss to coat. **(3)** Arrange the veggies in a single layer on a baking pan. **(4)** Cook, turning once, for 20 minutes or until soft and gently browned. **(5)** Take it out of the oven, put lemon juice all over it, and top it with fresh parsley. Keep heated before serving.

144. SPINACH AND AVOCADO SMOOTHIE

Total Time: 5 minutes | Prep Time: 5 minutes

Ingredients:

1 cup fresh spinach	½ ripe avocado
1 cup unsweetened almond milk	½ banana (for natural sweetness)
1 tbsp chia seeds	½ tsp vanilla extract
½ cup ice cubes (optional)	

Directions:

(1) Blend everything together. **(2)** Whisk or mix until combined. **(3)** Place in a glass and savor right away.

145. BAKED HERB-CRUSTED SALMON

Total Time: 25 minutes | Prep Time: 10 minutes

Ingredients:

2 salmon fillets (4-5 oz each)	1 tbsp olive oil
1 tbsp Dijon mustard	½ cup almond flour
1 tsp dried oregano	1 tsp dried basil
½ tsp garlic powder	½ tsp salt
¼ tsp black pepper	1 tsp lemon zest

Directions:

(1) Get your oven ready for 400°F or 200°C. Put parchment paper on a baking pan. **(2)** Dijon mustard and olive oil should be brushed onto the salmon fillets. **(3)** Combine the oregano, basil, almond flour, garlic powder, salt, pepper, and zest of the lemon in a bowl. **(4)** Apply a crust to the salmon fillets by pressing the herb mixture onto them. **(5)** Once the crust has become golden and opaque throughout, return the salmon fillets to the oven and cook for a further 12 to 15 minutes. Warm it up and serve it with some salad or roasted veggies on the side.

146. SESAME GINGER CUCUMBER SALAD

Total Time: 10 minutes | Prep Time: 10 minutes

Ingredients:

1 large cucumber, thinly sliced	1 tbsp sesame oil

1 tbsp rice vinegar	1 tsp low-sodium soy sauce or coconut aminos
½ tsp grated fresh ginger	1 tsp sesame seeds
1 green onion, sliced	½ tsp red pepper flakes (optional)

Directions:

(1) Mash the ginger, soy sauce, rice vinegar, and sesame oil in a mixing bowl. **(2)** Coat the cucumber slices equally by adding them and tossing them. **(3)** Prior to serving, garnish with sesame seeds, green onions, and red pepper flakes. **(4)** Give it 5 minutes to steep so the flavors can fully develop.

147. MEDITERRANEAN EGG MUFFINS

Total Time: 30 minutes | Prep Time: 10 minutes

Ingredients:

6 large eggs	¼ cup milk (or unsweetened almond milk)
½ cup feta cheese, crumbled	½ cup cherry tomatoes, diced
½ cup baby spinach, chopped	¼ cup red bell pepper, diced
¼ cup black olives, sliced	1 tsp dried oregano
½ tsp salt	¼ tsp black pepper
1 tbsp olive oil (for greasing)	

Directions:

(1) Set oven temperature to 375°F. Apply a little amount of olive oil to a muffin pan. **(2)** Merge the milk, eggs, salt, and pepper in a bowl and whisk to combine. **(3)** Mix in the oregano, feta cheese, bell pepper, cherry tomatoes, spinach, and black olives with the eggs. Combine by stirring. **(4)** Fill up every muffin pan cup about three-quarters of the way to the top with the batter. Fill the muffin pan equally. **(5)** After around 18 to 20 minutes in the oven, the eggs should be completely set and have a little golden hue to them. **(6)** After a few minutes, take it out of the pan and let it cool. Keep heated before serving.

148. GRILLED SALMON CAESAR SALAD

Total Time: 25 minutes | Prep Time: 10 minutes

Ingredients:

2 salmon fillets (about 6 oz each)	1 tbsp olive oil
½ tsp salt	¼ tsp black pepper
1 tsp garlic powder	1 tsp lemon juice
4 cups romaine lettuce, chopped	¼ cup Parmesan cheese, shredded
¼ cup croutons (optional)	¼ cup Caesar dressing (use a light or homemade version)
½ tsp Dijon mustard	

Directions:

(1) Turn the grill on high heat and let it heat up. **(2)** Before seasoning the salmon fillets with garlic powder, salt, and black pepper, brush them with olive oil. **(3)** Cook the salmon until it's flaky and cooked through, about 4 to 5 minutes, on each side of the grill. **(4)** Toss the romaine lettuce, croutons, and Parmesan cheese in a big dish. **(5)** Combine the Dijon mustard and Caesar dressing in a small dish. **(6)** After you've mixed the salad with the dressing, add the cooked salmon on top. Before serving, pour in some lemon juice.

149. AVOCADO BACON SALAD

Total Time: 20 minutes | Prep Time: 10 minutes

Ingredients:

4 cups mixed greens (arugula, spinach, or romaine)	1 ripe avocado, diced
4 strips of cooked bacon, crumbled	¼ cup cherry tomatoes, halved
¼ cup red onion, thinly sliced	¼ cup feta cheese (optional)
¼ cup almonds or walnuts, chopped	2 tbsp olive oil
1 tbsp balsamic vinegar	1 tsp Dijon mustard
½ tsp sal	¼ tsp black pepper

Directions:

(1) Gather the salad ingredients in a big basin and toss in the chopped nuts, avocado, cherry tomatoes, red onion, and mixed greens. *(2)* Dress the salad by combining the olive oil, balsamic vinegar, salt, black pepper, mustard, and mustard seeds in a small dish. *(3)* Lightly coat the salad with the dressing and toss to combine. *(4)* Serve right away with a sprinkle of crumbled bacon.

150. GRILLED LEMON SHRIMP SALAD

Total Time: 20 minutes | Prep Time: 10 minutes

Ingredients:

1 lb large shrimp, peeled and deveined	1 tbsp olive oil
1 tbsp lemon juice	1 tsp lemon zest
1 tsp garlic powder	½ tsp paprika
½ tsp salt	¼ tsp black pepper
4 cups mixed greens	½ cup cherry tomatoes, halved
¼ cup red onion, thinly sliced	¼ cup cucumbers, sliced
¼ cup feta cheese, crumbled	2 tbsp balsamic vinaigrette

Directions:

(1) The shrimp should be added to a bowl along with the chopped garlic, lemon juice, olive oil, salt, and pepper. Stir to combine. Bring an outside grill or pan to medium-high heat. *(2)* To get pink and fully cooked shrimp, grill for about 2 minutes on each side. Take it out of the oven. *(3)* Get a big bowl and toss in some feta cheese, cucumber, cherry tomatoes, red onion, and mixed greens. *(4)* After tossing with balsamic vinaigrette, sprinkle cooked shrimp over top. Make sure to serve right away.

151. GRILLED STEAK AND VEGGIE SKEWERS

Total Time: 30 minutes | Prep Time: 15 minutes

Ingredients:

1 lb sirloin steak, cut into cubes	1 zucchini, sliced
1 red bell pepper, cut into chunks	1 yellow bell pepper, cut into chunks
1 red onion, cut into chunks	1 cup cherry tomatoes
2 tbsp olive oil	1 tbsp balsamic vinegar
1 tsp garlic powder	1 tsp smoked paprika
Salt and black pepper to taste	Wooden or metal skewers

Directions:

(1) Turn the grill on high heat and let it heat up. *(2)* Olive oil, balsamic vinegar, garlic powder, smoked paprika, salt, and pepper should all be whisked together in a bowl. *(3)* Ten minutes before serving, toss the steak pieces and vegetables with the marinade. *(4)* Skewer the vegetables and Beef. *(5)* Turn the steak over after ten to twelve minutes on the grill or until done to your liking. *(6)* Accompany with a serving of cauliflower rice or leafy greens, and serve hot.

152. LEMON DILL ROASTED CHICKEN

Total Time: 50 minutes | Prep Time: 10 minutes

Ingredients:

4 bone-in, skin-on chicken thighs	2 tbsp olive oil
2 tbsp lemon juice	2 cloves garlic, minced
1 tsp dried dill	1 tsp onion powder
½ tsp salt	½ tsp black pepper
1 lemon, sliced	Fresh dill for garnish

Directions:

(1) Set oven temperature to 400°F. *(2)* In a little bowl, combine the olive oil, garlic powder, dried dill, salt, and pepper. Add the lemon juice and combine well. *(3)* After seasoning the chicken thighs, rub them with the mixture. *(4)* Arrange the chicken on a parchment-lined baking pan. Squeeze some lemon wedges on top. *(5)* Prior to serving, ensure the chicken reaches an internal temperature of 165 degrees Fahrenheit, typically achieved between 35 to 40 minutes of roasting. Add some fresh dill for garnish and pair it with some roasted veggies or a side salad.

153. AVOCADO LIME CHICKEN SALAD

Total Time: 15 minutes | Prep Time: 10 minutes

Ingredients:

2 cups cooked and shredded chicken breast	1 ripe avocado, mashed
2 tbsp lime juice	2 tbsp Greek yogurt (or mayo for a dairy-free option)
½ tsp garlic powder	½ tsp cumin
¼ tsp salt	¼ tsp black pepper
¼ cup chopped cilantro	¼ cup diced red onion
½ cup diced cucumber	½ cup cherry tomatoes, halved

Directions:

(1) The avocados and lime juice should be mashed together in a big basin until completely smooth. Greek yogurt, garlic powder, cumin, salt, and black pepper should be mixed together. *(2)* Chop some red onion, cucumber, cilantro, cherry tomatoes, and shredded chicken and toss it in. Thoroughly blend all ingredients. *(3)* Cold, wrap it in lettuce, put it on a bed of greens, or dip it into keto crackers.

154. KETO ZOODLE STIR-FRY

Total Time: 20 minutes | Prep Time: 10 minutes

Ingredients:

2 medium zucchinis, spiralized	1 tbsp olive oil
½ lb chicken breast sliced thin	1 red bell pepper, sliced
1 cup mushrooms, sliced	1 clove garlic, minced
1 tsp ginger, grated	2 tbsp coconut aminos (or low-sodium soy sauce)
½ tsp sesame oil	½ tsp red pepper flakes (optional)
1 tbsp sesame seeds for garnish	2 tbsp chopped green onions for garnish

Directions:

(1) After 5 or 6 minutes, add the chicken and simmer until done. Detach and put aside. *(2)* Toss in the mushrooms, garlic, ginger, and bell pepper in the same skillet. Add the garlic and

cook for another three to four minutes. **(3)** After 2 minutes of stirring, add the zucchini noodles. **(4)** Put the chicken back in the pan and season with red pepper flakes, sesame oil, and coconut aminos. Mix thoroughly. **(5)** Take the pan off the stove and add the green onions and sesame seeds as a garnish. Heat and serve immediately.

155. BAKED FETA AND SPINACH CASSEROLE

Total Time: 35 minutes | Prep Time: 10 minutes

Ingredients:

1 (8-ounce) block feta cheese	4 cups fresh spinach, chopped
1 cup cherry tomatoes, halved	2 cloves garlic, minced
2 tablespoons olive oil	½ teaspoon red pepper flakes
½ teaspoon dried oregano	¼ teaspoon salt
¼ teaspoon black pepper	2 eggs, lightly beaten
½ cup grated Parmesan cheese	

Directions:

(1) Get your oven preheated to 375°F, which is 190°C. Apply olive oil to a baking dish. **(2)** Add the garlic, cherry tomatoes, spinach, olive oil, oregano, salt, and black pepper to a big bowl. Season with red pepper flakes. **(3)** In a baking dish, distribute the ingredients uniformly. Put the feta chunk in the middle. **(4)** To make the feta melt and the spinach wilt, bake for 20 minutes. **(5)** After removing from the oven, mix the ingredients together carefully. Before topping with Parmesan, whisk in the beaten eggs. **(6)** Once the eggs have set and the top has become a golden brown color, bake for a further 10 minutes. **(7)** Allow it to cool for a short while before consumption.

156. SHRIMP AND AVOCADO SALAD

Total Time: 20 minutes | Prep Time: 10 minutes

Ingredients:

1 pound cooked shrimp, peeled and deveined	1 avocado, diced
1 cup cherry tomatoes, halved	¼ cup red onion, finely chopped
¼ cup fresh cilantro, chopped	Juice of 1 lime
2 tablespoons olive oil	½ teaspoon salt
¼ teaspoon black pepper	½ teaspoon cumin

Directions:

(1) Combine the shrimp, avocado, cherry tomatoes, red onion, and cilantro in a big bowl. **(2)** In a small bowl, mix together the cumin, olive oil, salt, pepper, and lime juice. Gently mix the salad ingredients after drizzling the dressing over them. **(3)** The flavors will meld after 5 to 10 minutes of sitting. **(4)** Top with more cilantro, if preferred, and serve right away.

157. CHEESY CAULIFLOWER CASSEROLE

Total Time: 40 minutes | Prep Time: 10 minutes

Ingredients:

1 medium head cauliflower, cut into florets	1 cup shredded cheddar cheese
½ cup grated	½ cup Greek yogurt

Parmesan cheese
¼ cup heavy cream
½ teaspoon onion powder
¼ teaspoon black pepper
¼ cup breadcrumbs (optional)
2 cloves garlic, minced
½ teaspoon salt
¼ teaspoon paprika
1 tablespoon butter, melted

Directions:

(1) Get your oven preheated to 375°F, which is 190°C. Spray cooking spray lightly onto a baking dish. **(2)** Grill the cauliflower florets for 5 to 7 minutes or until they are soft. Thoroughly empty the drain. **(3)** Greek yogurt, heavy cream, garlic powder, onion powder, salt, black pepper, and paprika should all be combined in a big basin. Then, combine the Parmesan and cheddar cheeses. **(4)** Toss in the cauliflower and coat it well. Put the baking dish in the oven. **(5)** If desired, top the casserole with a mixture of breadcrumbs and melted butter, which should be kept in a small basin. **(6)** Once bubbling and golden brown, bake for 20 to 25 minutes. **(7)** Allow it to cool for a short while before consumption.

158. LEMON HERB CRUSTED SALMON

Total Time: 25 minutes | Prep Time: 10 minutes

Ingredients:

4 salmon fillets (6 ounces each)
2 tablespoons Dijon mustard
2 tablespoons lemon juice
¼ cup grated Parmesan cheese
1 teaspoon dried parsley
2 tablespoons olive oil
1 teaspoon lemon zest
½ cup almond flour
1 teaspoon dried oregano
½ teaspoon garlic powder
½ teaspoon salt
¼ teaspoon black pepper

Directions:

(1) Set oven temperature to 400°F. Sprinkle parchment paper on a baking pan. **(2)** Combine lemon juice, zest, and Dijon mustard in a small dish. **(3)** Salt, pepper, garlic powder, oregano, almond flour, parsley, and Parmesan are to be mixed in a separate basin. **(4)** Spread the herb-almond flour mixture evenly over the salmon fillets, then brush with the mustard mixture. **(5)** Season the fillets with olive oil and arrange them on a baking pan. **(6)** Cook in the oven for 12–15 minutes or until the crust becomes golden and the salmon turns flaky. **(7)** Warm it up and serve it with some salad or veggies.

159. AVOCADO DEVILED EGGS

Total Time: 25 minutes | Prep Time: 15 minutes | Cook Time: 10 minutes

Ingredients:

6 large eggs
1 tbsp lemon juice
1/4 tsp garlic powder
1/4 tsp black pepper
1/4 tsp paprika (for garnish)
1 ripe avocado
1/2 tsp Dijon mustard
1/4 tsp salt
1 tbsp chopped fresh cilantro or parsley

Directions:

(1) Get some water boiling in a saucepan. Boil some water and gently add the eggs; simmer for 10 minutes. **(2)** Before peeling, remove the eggs from the water and cool them in an ice bath for five minutes. **(3)** Cut eggs lengthwise in half and scoop out the yolks. **(4)** Combine avocado, lemon juice, Dijon mustard, garlic powder, salt, and black pepper in a bowl with the yolks and mash until smooth. **(5)** Add the mixture to the egg whites again using a spoon or a pipette. **(6)** Add a dash of paprika and some chopped parsley or cilantro for garnish. **(7)** Keep it in the fridge until serving time, or serve it right away.

160. GARLIC PARMESAN KALE CHIPS

Total Time: 20 minutes | Prep Time: 5 minutes | Cook Time: 15 minutes

Ingredients:

1 bunch of kale, stems removed	1 tbsp olive oil
1/2 tsp garlic powder	1/4 tsp salt
1/4 tsp black pepper	2 tbsp grated Parmesan cheese

Directions:

(1) Preheating the oven to 300°F is highly recommended. In a large bowl, combine the fresh kale, garlic powder, olive oil, salt, & black pepper. Whisk to combine. **(2)** Toss the kale to coat before placing it in a single layer on a baking sheet. **(3)** Cook for 12–15 minutes, turning once, or until golden and crisp. **(4)** Top with grated Parmesan and serve while still warm.

161. LEMON THYME ROASTED VEGGIES

Total Time: 35 minutes | Prep Time: 10 minutes | Cook Time: 25 minutes

Ingredients:

1 zucchini, chopped	1 red bell pepper, chopped
1 cup cherry tomatoes	1 small red onion, sliced
2 tbsp olive oil	1 tbsp lemon juice
1 tsp fresh thyme leaves	1/2 tsp salt
1/4 tsp black pepper	1/2 tsp garlic powder

Directions:

(1) Set oven temperature to 400°F. **(2)** Combine the bell pepper, red onion, cherry tomatoes, zucchini, and lemon juice in a large bowl with the thyme, olive oil, salt, pepper, and garlic powder. **(3)** Arrange the veggies on a baking pan in one even layer. **(4)** Cook, stirring once halfway through, for 25 minutes or until soft and slightly browned. **(5)** Toss warm with a salad or serve as a side dish.

162. LOW-CARB SHEPHERD'S PIE

Total Time: 50 minutes | Prep Time: 15 minutes | Cook Time: 35 minutes

Ingredients:

For the filling:

1 lb ground turkey or Beef	1/2 onion, diced
2 cloves garlic, minced	1 cup chopped mushrooms
1 cup chopped cauliflower	1/2 cup beef or chicken broth
1 tsp Worcestershire sauce	1/2 tsp salt
1/4 tsp black pepper	1/2 tsp dried thyme

For the topping:

1 medium head cauliflower, chopped	2 tbsp butter
1/4 cup grated Parmesan cheese	1/2 tsp garlic powder
1/4 tsp salt	

Directions:

(1) Get your oven preheated to 375°F, which is 190°C. **(2)** Mash the softened cauliflower with the butter, Parmesan, garlic powder, and salt after steaming it. Remove off the table. **(3)** Brown ground beef & turkey in a pan over medium heat. Get rid of any extra fat. **(4)** Toss in the chopped cauliflower, mushrooms, garlic, onion, and garlic powder into the pan. Make sure to cook for at least 5 minutes. **(5)** Add the broth, Worcestershire sauce, pepper, salt, and thyme, and stir to combine. Low heat for five minutes. **(6)** Place the beef blend in an ovenproof dish. On top, distribute the mashed cauliflower in a uniform layer. **(7)** After 20 minutes in the oven, you should see a little goldening on top. **(8)** Allow it to cool for a short while before consumption.

163. LOW-CARB BAKED ZITI

Total Time: 40 minutes | Prep Time: 15 minutes

Ingredients:

1 lb ground turkey or Beef	1 cup marinara sauce (sugar-free)
1 medium spaghetti squash, cooked and shredded	1 cup ricotta cheese
1 cup shredded mozzarella cheese	¼ cup grated Parmesan cheese
1 tsp garlic powder	1 tsp Italian seasoning
½ tsp salt	½ tsp black pepper
1 tbsp olive oil	

Directions:

(1) Get your oven preheated to 375°F, which is 190°C. **(2)** Melt the olive oil in a pan set over medium heat. Before browning, add ground beef or turkey. Get rid of any extra fat. **(3)** Garlic powder, Italian seasoning, salt, pepper, and marinara sauce should be stirred in. Low heat for five minutes. **(4)** Shred the spaghetti squash and mix it with the ricotta cheese in a bowl. **(5)** Divide the beef sauce in half and spread it onto a baking dish. Spread the squash-ricotta mixture on top. Garnish with the leftover meat sauce. **(6)** Top with a generous amount of Parmesan and mozzarella. **(7)** Put it in the oven and let it melt and bubble for about 20 minutes. Allow it to cool for a little before you eat it.

164. ZOODLE VEGGIE STIR-FRY

Total Time: 20 minutes | Prep Time: 10 minutes

Ingredients:

2 medium zucchinis, spiralized into noodles (zoodles)	½ cup bell peppers, thinly sliced
½ cup broccoli florets	½ cup mushrooms, sliced
2 tbsp coconut aminos or soy sauce	1 tbsp olive oil
1 clove garlic, minced	½ tsp ginger, grated
½ tsp red pepper flakes (optional)	1 tbsp sesame seeds (for garnish)
1 green onion, sliced (for garnish)	

Directions:

(1) Toss the olive oil into a large pan and heat it over medium-high heat. Simmer for 30 seconds after adding ginger and garlic. **(2)** Incorporate broccoli, mushrooms, and bell peppers. Gently cook for three to four minutes or until just beginning to soften. **(3)** Toss in the zoodles and vegan aminos. After two more minutes of cooking, toss to mix. **(4)** After taking it off the fire, top it with chopped green onion and sesame seeds. **(5)** Quickly serve as a low-carb, light lunch.

165. LOW-CARB CRAB CAKES

Total Time: 25 minutes | Prep Time: 10 minutes

Ingredients:

- 8 oz lump crab meat
- 1 egg, beaten
- 1 tbsp Dijon mustard
- ½ tsp garlic powder
- ¼ tsp black pepper
- 1 tbsp fresh parsley, chopped (for garnish)
- ¼ cup almond flour
- 2 tbsp mayonnaise
- ½ tsp Old Bay seasoning
- ¼ tsp salt
- 2 tbsp coconut oil (for frying)

Directions:

(1) Combine the crab meat, almond flour, egg, mayonnaise, Dijon mustard, Old Bay seasoning, garlic powder, salt, and pepper in a bowl. Add the Old Bay spice and stir. **(2)** Shape into little patties, about four. **(3)** Coconut oil should be warmed in a pan over medium heat. **(4)** Brown and crisp the crab cakes in a pan by frying them for three to four minutes on each side. **(5)** Take it out of the pan and set it on paper towels to drain. **(6)** A touch of lemon and some fresh parsley make a lovely garnish.

166. KETO SPINACH ARTICHOKE DIP

Total Time: 30 minutes | Prep Time: 10 minutes

Ingredients:

- 1 cup fresh spinach, chopped
- 4 oz cream cheese, softened
- ½ cup shredded mozzarella cheese
- 1 tsp garlic powder
- ½ tsp salt
- ½ cup canned artichoke hearts, chopped
- ½ cup sour cream
- ¼ cup grated Parmesan cheese
- ½ tsp onion powder
- ¼ tsp black pepper

Directions:

(1) Preheat oven to 375°F (190°C). **(2)** Cream cheese and mozzarella should be mixed together in a bowl. **(3)** Garlic powder, onion powder, artichoke hearts, spinach, and salt & pepper are added after seasoning. **(4)** Bake for 15 to 20 minutes, or until bubbling and golden, in an oven-safe dish. Serve warm with keto-friendly crackers or fresh veggie sticks.

167. ROASTED GARLIC AND HERB CAULIFLOWER

Total Time: 35 minutes | Prep Time: 10 minutes

Ingredients:

- 1 head cauliflower, cut into florets
- 2 tbsp olive oil
- 1 tsp dried thyme
- ½ tsp black pepper
- 2 tbsp grated Parmesan cheese (optional)
- 3 cloves garlic, minced
- 1 tsp dried oregano
- ½ tsp salt
- 1 tbsp lemon juice

Directions:

(1) Set the oven temperature to 400°F. Sprinkle parchment paper on a baking pan. **(2)** Olive oil, minced garlic, oregano, thyme, salt, and black pepper should be mixed with the cauliflower florets in a big bowl. **(3)** Even distribute the cauliflower on the prepared baking sheet. **(4)** To get a golden brown and soft texture, roast for 25 minutes while stirring once halfway through. **(5)** After taking it out of the oven, top with lemon juice and, if desired, Parmesan cheese. **(6)** Warm it up and savor it!

168. LOW-CARB TORTILLA SOUP

Total Time: 30 minutes | Prep Time: 10 minutes

Ingredients:

1 tbsp olive oil	½ onion, diced
2 cloves garlic, minced	1 tsp cumin
1 tsp chili powder	½ tsp smoked paprika
1 (14.5 oz) can diced tomatoes	4 cups chicken broth
1 cup shredded cooked chicken	1 small zucchini, spiralized or diced
½ cup chopped bell peppers	½ avocado, diced
¼ cup fresh cilantro, chopped	1 lime, cut into wedges

Directions:

(1) The best way to heat olive oil is in a large pot over medium heat. Sauté the garlic and onion until they release their aroma. **(2)** Combine smoked paprika, chili powder, cumin, and stir. Add 30 more seconds of cooking time. **(3)** Toss in the chicken stock and chopped tomatoes. Simmer for 10 minutes after bringing to a boil. **(4)** Toss in some bell peppers, zucchini, and shredded chicken. Add five more minutes of simmering time. **(5)** Before serving, reheat and top with sliced avocado, cilantro, and lime juice.

169. ALMOND-CRUSTED BAKED CHICKEN

Total Time: 35 minutes | Prep Time: 10 minutes

Ingredients:

2 boneless, skinless chicken breasts	½ cup almond flour
½ cup crushed almonds	1 tsp garlic powder
1 tsp paprika	½ tsp salt
½ tsp black pepper	1 egg, beaten
1 tbsp olive oil	

Directions:

(1) Get your oven preheated to 375°F, which is 190°C. Sprinkle parchment paper on a baking pan. **(2)** Make a shallow dish and mix together almond flour, crushed almonds, garlic powder, paprika, salt, and black pepper. Before coating with the almond mixture, dip each chicken breast in the beaten egg. **(3)** Drizzle olive oil over the chicken before placing it on the baking sheet. **(4)** The chicken should be cooked through and golden brown after 25 minutes in the oven. **(5)** After 5 minutes, let aside to cool before cutting. Pair it with the low-carb veggies that you choose.

170. ZOODLE PRIMAVERA

Total Time: 20 minutes | Prep Time: 10 minutes

Ingredients:

2 medium zucchini, spiralized	1 tbsp olive oil
1 clove garlic, minced	½ cup cherry tomatoes, halved
½ red bell pepper, sliced	¼ cup fresh basil, chopped
¼ tsp red pepper flakes (optional)	¼ cup grated Parmesan cheese (optional)

Directions:

(1) Spread out the olive oil and set it over medium heat in a large pan. For 30 seconds, sauté the garlic. **(2)** Bell pepper and cherry tomatoes should be added. Soften by cooking for three to four minutes. **(3)** Add the zucchini noodles and continue cooking for an additional 2 minutes or until they are almost soft. **(4)** If desired, add red pepper flakes and fresh basil and stir to combine. **(5)** Take it off the stove and, if you want, top it with Parmesan. **(6)** This fresh and light low-carb meal is ready to be served right away.

171. SPINACH AND FETA STUFFED PEPPERS

Total Time: 40 minutes | Prep Time: 15 minutes

Ingredients:

- 4 large bell peppers (any color), halved
- ½ cup feta cheese, crumbled
- 1 small onion, finely chopped
- 1 tablespoon olive oil
- ½ teaspoon black pepper
- ¼ teaspoon red pepper flakes (optional)
- 1 cup fresh spinach, chopped
- 1 cup cooked quinoa or cauliflower rice
- 2 cloves garlic, minced
- ½ teaspoon dried oregano
- ¼ teaspoon salt

Directions:

(1) Set oven temperature to 375°F. Spread parchment paper on a baking dish. **(2)** Grease a pan and place it on a medium heat setting. Flavor the mixture by adding the garlic and onions and sautéing for 2 minutes. **(3)** Incorporate the spinach after cooking for a minute or two, stirring occasionally or until it begins to wilt. Take the pan off the stove and combine the quinoa, feta cheese, oregano, salt, black pepper, red pepper flakes, and oregano. **(4)** Put half of the spinach mixture and half of the feta mixture into each bell pepper. **(5)** To get the peppers soft, fill them and bake them in an uncovered baking tray for 20 to 25 minutes. Warm it up and savor it!

172. PARMESAN CRUSTED CHICKEN TENDERS

Total Time: 30 minutes | Prep Time: 10 minutes

Ingredients:

- 1 lb chicken tenders
- ½ cup almond flour (or breadcrumbs for a crunchier texture)
- ½ teaspoon smoked paprika
- ½ teaspoon black pepper
- 2 tablespoons olive oil
- ½ cup grated Parmesan cheese
- 1 teaspoon garlic powder
- ½ teaspoon salt
- 1 large egg, beaten

Directions:

(1) If baking, preheat oven to 400°F or 200°C. To fry, put oil in a pan and set it over medium heat. **(2)** Whisk the egg in a separate dish. Toss together almond flour, Parmesan, garlic powder, paprika, salt, and black pepper in yet another bowl. **(3)** Before even coating with the Parmesan mixture, dip each chicken piece into the egg. **(4)** Bake, uncovered, for 18 to 20 minutes, turning once, or until done. Lay out on a parchment-lined baking sheet. **(5)** If you want to fry your tenders, give them three to four minutes on each side until they're cooked through and golden brown. **(6)** Light salad or sugar-free dipping sauce would be a good accompaniment.

173. BROCCOLI CHEDDAR SOUP

Total Time: 35 minutes | Prep Time: 10 minutes

Ingredients:

- 2 cups fresh broccoli florets
- 2 cloves garlic, minced
- 1 cup shredded sharp cheddar cheese
- 1 tablespoon butter
- 1 small onion, chopped
- 2 cups unsweetened almond milk (or low-sodium chicken broth)
- ½ cup heavy cream
- ½ teaspoon salt

| ½ teaspoon black pepper | ¼ teaspoon ground nutmeg (optional) |

Directions:

(1) In a tall saucepan set over medium heat, melt the butter. Soften the garlic and onion by gently sautéing them in a skillet. **(2)** Sauté the broccoli florets for three minutes, tossing them around every so often. **(3)** Add the almond milk and whisk while reducing heat to low. Ten to twelve minutes, covered, should be enough time for the broccoli to soften. **(4)** Smooth down the soup by blending it all at once or in portions with an immersion blender. **(5)** Put it back on the stove and mix in the nutmeg, salt, pepper, cheddar cheese, heavy cream, and black pepper. While the soup is thickening, melt the cheese. **(6)** Top with more cheese or chopped chives, and serve hot.

174. LEMON GARLIC BUTTER SCALLOPS

Total Time: 15 minutes | Prep Time: 5 minutes

Ingredients:

1 lb sea scallops, patted dry	2 tablespoons butter
1 tablespoon olive oil	2 cloves garlic, minced
Juice of 1 lemon	½ teaspoon salt
½ teaspoon black pepper	¼ teaspoon red pepper flakes (optional)
1 tablespoon fresh parsley, chopped	

Directions:

(1) Over medium-high heat, melt one tablespoon of olive oil & 1 tablespoon of butter in a large pan. The scallops should be seasoned with black pepper and salt. **(2)** To get a golden brown color, saute the scallops in a pan for two to three minutes on each side. Lift out of the pan and place aside. **(3)** Turn the heat down to medium and stir in the remaining garlic and butter. To release the aroma, sauté for 30 seconds. **(4)** Blend in the zest of the lemon and the chile pepper. Spoon sauce over the scallops before returning them to the pan. **(5)** Take it off the stove, top it with some fresh parsley, and serve it hot.

175. SPAGHETTI SQUASH ZOODLE COMBO

Total Time: 40 minutes | Prep Time: 15 minutes

Ingredients:

1 medium spaghetti squash	1 medium zucchini, spiralized
1 tbsp olive oil	2 cloves garlic, minced
½ tsp sea salt	¼ tsp black pepper
¼ tsp red pepper flakes (optional)	½ cup cherry tomatoes, halved
¼ cup grated Parmesan cheese	1 tbsp fresh basil, chopped

Directions:

(1) Set oven temperature to 400°F. After halving the spaghetti squash lengthwise, remove its seeds. **(2)** Sprinkle with salt & pepper and drizzle with half a tablespoon of olive oil. Roast, cut side down, for 30 minutes or until soft when prodded with a fork. **(3)** Toss the remaining olive oil into a pan and set it over medium heat while the squash roasts. Sauté the garlic until it releases its aroma. **(4)** Toss in with cherry tomatoes, spiralized zucchini, and red pepper flakes. Stir periodically while cooking for 2 to 3 minutes. **(5)** When the spaghetti squash is cooked through, remove its flesh using a fork to make "noodles" and put them in the pan. Combine all of the ingredients. **(6)** Before serving, sprinkle with fresh basil and Parmesan cheese.

176. CHEESY ZUCCHINI BOATS

Total Time: 35 minutes | Prep Time: 10 minutes

Ingredients:

2 medium zucchinis, halved lengthwise	½ cup cooked ground turkey or chicken
½ cup marinara sauce (sugar-free)	½ tsp garlic powder
½ tsp Italian seasoning	¼ tsp salt
¼ cup shredded mozzarella cheese	1 tbsp grated Parmesan cheese
1 tbsp fresh parsley, chopped	

Directions:

(1) Get your oven preheated to 375°F, which is 190°C. Cut the zucchini in half lengthwise and scoop out the middle, making a boat shape. **(2)** Blend cooked ground turkey with marinara sauce, garlic powder, Italian seasoning, & salt in a bowl. **(3)** Spoon the filling into the zucchini halves that have been hollowed out. **(4)** Top with a sprinkle of Parmesan and mozzarella. **(5)** After twenty to twenty-five minutes in the oven, the cheese should be melted and bubbling. **(6)** Warm and top with fresh parsley.

177. BACON-WRAPPED PORK TENDERLOIN

Total Time: 45 minutes | Prep Time: 15 minutes

Ingredients:

1 lb pork tenderloin	6-8 slices of bacon
1 tbsp olive oil	1 tsp smoked paprika
½ tsp garlic powder	½ tsp onion powder
½ tsp salt	¼ tsp black pepper
1 tbsp Dijon mustard	

Directions:

(1) Set oven temperature to 400°F. **(2)** A little bowl should be enough to mix the smoked paprika, smashed garlic, chopped onion, olive oil, salt, and pepper. The pork tenderloin should be rubbed with the spice mixture. For added taste, brush with Dijon mustard. **(3)** Carefully round the pig with bacon pieces, being sure to slightly overlap them. Use toothpicks to secure if necessary. **(4)** Arrange the pork on a parchment-lined baking pan. Bring the internal temperature to 145°F after 35–40 minutes in the oven. **(5)** After 5 minutes, set aside time to rest, then cut and serve.

178. LOW-CARB CHICKEN TACO SKILLET

Total Time: 25 minutes | Prep Time: 10 minutes

Ingredients:

1 lb boneless, skinless chicken breasts, diced	1 tbsp olive oil
½ tsp salt	½ tsp black pepper
1 tsp chili powder	½ tsp cumin
½ tsp smoked paprika	¼ tsp garlic powder
½ cup diced bell peppers	½ cup diced onions
½ cup diced tomatoes	½ cup shredded cheddar cheese
¼ cup fresh cilantro, chopped	1 avocado, sliced (optional)

Directions:

(1) Spread out the olive oil and set it over medium heat in a large pan. Salt, pepper, cumin, garlic powder, smoked paprika, and chili powder should be added to the chopped chicken. Stir periodically while it cooks for 5-7 minutes. *(2)* Toss in some chopped tomatoes, onions, and bell peppers. To get soft veggies, continue cooking for an additional 5 minutes. *(3)* To melt the cheddar cheese, cover the pan and sprinkle it on top. *(4)* Accompany with slices of avocado and top with chopped fresh cilantro.

179. BAKED HERB CHICKEN WINGS

Total Time: 45 minutes | Prep Time: 10 minutes

Ingredients:

2 lbs chicken wings	2 tbsp olive oil
1 tsp sea salt	½ tsp black pepper
1 tsp garlic powder	1 tsp onion powder
1 tsp smoked paprika	1 tsp dried oregano
1 tsp dried thyme	½ tsp cayenne pepper (optional)
1 tbsp lemon juice	

Directions:

(1) Turn the oven on high heat to 400°F. Put a wire rack or parchment paper on a baking pan. *(2)* Add the olive oil, pepper, salt, garlic powder, onion powder, smoked paprika, oregano, thyme, and cayenne pepper to a big bowl. Stir to combine. *(3)* Toss in the chicken wings to coat them evenly. *(4)* Lay out the wings on the baking sheet in a single layer. Turn the pan halfway during baking time. Bake for 35 to 40 minutes. *(5)* Serve hot after removing it from the oven and drizzling it with lemon juice.

180. CREAMY LEMON ZOODLE ALFREDO

Total Time: 20 minutes | Prep Time: 10 minutes

Ingredients:

2 medium zucchini, spiralized	1 tbsp olive oil
2 cloves garlic, minced	1 cup unsweetened coconut milk
½ cup grated Parmesan cheese	1 tbsp lemon juice
1 tsp lemon zest	½ tsp sea salt
¼ tsp black pepper	¼ tsp crushed red pepper flakes (optional)
Fresh parsley for garnish	

Directions:

(1) Oil a skillet & set it over medium heat. Sauté minced garlic for 30 seconds or until it begins to release its aroma. *(2)* Simmer after adding coconut milk. Add the Parmesan, lemon zest, salt, and black pepper and mix well. Simmer for three to four minutes or until only a thin consistency remains. *(3)* Toss in the spiralized zucchini and mix one more to combine. Just until softened, cook for two to three minutes. *(4)* Serve right away after removing from heat; top with chopped fresh parsley.

181. LEMON THYME GRILLED CHICKEN

Total Time: 30 minutes | Prep Time: 10 minutes

Ingredients:

2 boneless, skinless chicken breasts	2 tbsp olive oil
1 tbsp fresh lemon juice	1 tsp lemon zest
1 tsp dried thyme	1 tsp garlic powder
½ tsp sea salt	¼ tsp black pepper
½ tsp smoked paprika	

Directions:

(1) Combine the olive oil, smoked paprika, black pepper, garlic powder, thyme, lemon

zest, lemon juice, and lemon in a small bowl. *(2)* For a minimum of fifteen minutes, coat the chicken breasts with the marinade. *(3)* Get a grill or pan ready by heating it to medium-high. *(4)* To get a chicken's internal temperature of 165°F (75°C), grill it for 5 to 7 minutes on each side. *(5)* After 5 minutes, let aside to cool before cutting. Platter hot and accompany with a side salad or vegetables.

182. KETO CAULIFLOWER FRIED RICE

Total Time: 20 minutes | Prep Time: 10 minutes

Ingredients:

2 cups riced cauliflower	1 tbsp olive oil
2 eggs, beaten	½ cup diced bell peppers
½ cup chopped green onions	½ cup diced mushroom
1 tbsp coconut aminos (or low-sodium soy sauce)	½ tsp garlic powder
½ tsp onion powder	¼ tsp sea salt
¼ tsp black pepper	½ tsp sesame oil

Directions:

(1) Grease a pan and place it on a medium heat setting. Sauté the mushrooms and bell peppers for three to four minutes. *(2)* Move the veggies to the side of the skillet. Before adding the eggs, scramble them until they're fully cooked. *(3)* Include green onions, riced cauliflower, coconut aminos, garlic powder, onion powder, salt, and pepper. Mix thoroughly. *(4)* Cauliflower needs a further four to five minutes in the pan to get tenderness. *(5)* Pour sesame oil over the top just before serving.

183. ZUCCHINI LASAGNA ROLLS

Total Time: 45 minutes | Prep Time: 20 minutes

Ingredients:

2 large zucchinis, thinly sliced lengthwise	1 cup ricotta cheese
½ cup shredded mozzarella cheese	¼ cup grated Parmesan cheese
1 egg	½ teaspoon garlic powder
½ teaspoon Italian seasoning	1 cup sugar-free marinara sauce
1 tablespoon olive oil	Salt and pepper, to taste

Directions:

(1) Warm the oven to 375 degrees Fahrenheit. A baking dish should be lightly greased. *(2)* Use a mandoline or a sharp knife to thinly slice the zucchini. *(3)* Combine the ricotta, mozzarella, Parmesan, egg, garlic powder, Italian seasoning, salt, & pepper in a bowl. *(4)* Roll up the zucchini strips firmly after spreading one spoonful of stuffing over each one. *(5)* In a baking dish, spread the marinara sauce and arrange the rolls seam-side down. *(6)* Olive oil and more mozzarella, if desired, drizzle over the dish. *(7)* The cheese should be bubbling and brown after 25 minutes in the oven. Warm it up before serving.

184. ASIAN CHICKEN CABBAGE STIR-FRY

Total Time: 25 minutes | Prep Time: 10 minutes

Ingredients:

1 lb boneless, skinless chicken	2 cups shredded cabbage

breast
1 red bell pepper, julienned
1 tablespoon ginger, grated
1 tablespoon sesame oil
½ teaspoon red pepper flakes (optional)
2 green onions, chopped
2 cloves garlic, minced
2 tablespoons coconut aminos
1 teaspoon rice vinegar
1 tablespoon sesame seeds

Directions:

(1) Put the sesame oil into a pan and heat it over medium-high heat briefly. After 5 or 6 minutes, add the chicken and cook until it's browned. *(2)* After one more minute of cooking, or until aromatic, stir in the garlic and ginger, cook the bell pepper and cabbage for a further four to five minutes or until they are tender-crisp. *(3)* Add the rice vinegar, red pepper flakes, and coconut aminos and mix well. Continue cooking while stirring constantly for an additional two minutes. *(4)* Take the pan off the stove and add the green onions and sesame seeds as a garnish. Heat and serve immediately.

185. CREAMY TOMATO BASIL SOUP

Total Time: 30 minutes | Prep Time: 10 minutes

Ingredients:

1 tablespoon olive oil
2 cloves garlic, minced
2 cups vegetable broth
¼ teaspoon red pepper flakes (optional)
½ cup fresh basil leaves, chopped
1 small onion, chopped
1 (28-ounce) can crushed tomatoes
1 teaspoon Italian seasoning
½ cup unsweetened almond milk
Salt and pepper, to taste

Directions:

(1) Put the olive oil in a pot and place it over medium heat. After 3–4 minutes, add the onion and simmer until it becomes tender. *(2)* Sauté the garlic for a further minute. *(3)* Red pepper flakes, Italian seasoning, vegetable broth, and smashed tomatoes, stir to combine. After 15 minutes, reduce heat to low. *(4)* Mix the almond milk with the fresh basil in a blender or food processor. Mix until combined. *(5)* Dress it with a pinch of salt and pepper just before serving.

186. ROASTED GARLIC ZOODLE SALAD

Total Time: 20 minutes | Prep Time: 10 minutes

Ingredients:

2 medium zucchini, spiralized
2 tablespoons olive oil
1 teaspoon Dijon mustard
¼ teaspoon black pepper
¼ cup feta cheese (optional)
1 head of garlic, roasted
1 tablespoon lemon juice
½ teaspoon salt
¼ cup cherry tomatoes, halved
2 tablespoons chopped parsley

Directions:

(1) Set oven temperature to 400°F. Peel the garlic cloves, rub them with olive oil, place them in a foil packet, and roast them for half an hour. Allow to cool. *(2)* Transfer the roasted garlic cloves to a small bowl and crush them with a fork. *(3)* Toss in the dressing, which consists of olive oil, lemon juice, Dijon mustard, pepper, and salt. Cherry tomatoes, spiralized zucchini, feta (if used), and parsley are to be mixed together. *(4)* Mix with the

roasted garlic vinaigrette and serve right away.

187. JALAPEÑO POPPER STUFFED MUSHROOMS

Total Time: 30 minutes | Prep Time: 10 minutes | Cook Time: 20 minutes

Ingredients:

12 large cremini or button mushrooms, stems removed	4 oz cream cheese, softened
½ cup shredded cheddar cheese	2 jalapeños, finely diced (seeds removed for less heat)
2 strips of cooked turkey bacon, crumbled	¼ tsp garlic powder
¼ tsp smoked paprika	Salt and pepper, to taste
1 tbsp olive oil	

Directions:

(1) Set oven temperature to 375°F. **(2)** To remove the mushroom stems, wet a paper towel and set it aside. Combine chopped jalapeños, turkey bacon, cream cheese, cheddar cheese, garlic powder, smoked paprika, salt, and pepper in a bowl. **(3)** Put a little of the cheese mixture into each mushroom cap. **(4)** Before placing the mushrooms on a baking pan, brush them with olive oil. **(5)** Grill for 18 to 20 minutes or until the top is brown and the mixture bubbles slightly. **(6)** Warm it up and savor it!

188. ZOODLE STIR-FRY WITH PORK

Total Time: 25 minutes | Prep Time: 10 minutes | Cook Time: 15 minutes

Ingredients:

2 medium zucchini, spiralized into zoodles	½ lb lean pork tenderloin, thinly sliced
1 tbsp avocado oil	½ cup bell peppers, sliced
½ cup broccoli florets	2 cloves garlic, minced
1 tsp grated ginger	2 tbsp coconut aminos
1 tbsp rice vinegar	½ tsp sesame oil
1 tsp sesame seeds (for garnish)	1 green onion, sliced

Directions:

(1) In a big skillet, heat the avocado oil over medium-high heat. **(2)** Flip the pork slices over and heat for another 3 to 4 minutes or until they are browned. Detach and put aside. **(3)** Toss in the broccoli, garlic, ginger, and bell peppers in the same skillet. Cook, stirring occasionally, for three minutes. **(4)** With the zoodles, coconut aminos, rice vinegar, and sesame oil, go into the mixture. Sauté for a further two minutes. **(5)** After a minute of cooking, add the pork back to the pan and mix everything together. **(6)** Add green onions and sesame seeds as garnishes. Make sure to serve right away.

189. EGGPLANT ZOODLE PARMESAN

Total Time: 35 minutes | Prep Time: 10 minutes | Cook Time: 25 minutes

Ingredients:

1 medium eggplant, sliced into ½-inch rounds	2 medium zucchini, spiralized into zoodles
1 cup marinara sauce (sugar-free)	½ cup shredded mozzarella cheese
¼ cup grated Parmesan cheese	1 egg, beaten
½ cup almond flour	1 tsp Italian seasoning
½ tsp garlic powder	Salt and pepper, to

1 tbsp olive oil taste

Lemon wedges for serving

Directions:

(1) Set the oven temperature to 400°F. Sprinkle parchment paper on a baking pan. **(2)** To remove excess water, sprinkle salt over the eggplant slices and let them for 10 minutes. Pat dry. **(3)** Coat each slice with a mixture of almond flour, Italian seasoning, garlic powder, and beaten egg. **(4)** Oil a skillet & set it over medium heat. After two or three minutes in the pan, flip the eggplant slices and cook until golden. **(5)** After transferring the eggplant to the baking sheet, sprinkle mozzarella, Parmesan, and marinara sauce over top. **(6)** The cheese should be bubbling and brown after 15 minutes in the oven. **(7)** At the same time, soften the zoodles by sautéing them in a skillet for 2 minutes. **(8)** Top zoodles with eggplant and dig in!

190. GREEK TURKEY MEATBALL BOWLS

Total Time: 30 minutes | Prep Time: 10 minutes | Cook Time: 20 minutes

Ingredients:

For the meatballs:

1 lb ground turkey	¼ cup almond flour
1 egg, beaten	1 tsp oregano
½ tsp garlic powder	½ tsp onion powder
½ tsp salt	¼ tsp black pepper
1 tbsp olive oil	

For the bowls:

2 cups cauliflower rice, cooked	½ cup cherry tomatoes, halved
½ cup cucumber, diced	¼ cup crumbled feta cheese
2 tbsp tzatziki sauce	1 tbsp fresh dill, chopped

Directions:

(1) Set oven temperature to 400°F. Sprinkle parchment paper on a baking pan. **(2)** The almond flour, ground turkey, pepper, egg, oregano, garlic powder, onion powder, and salt should all be combined in a basin. Put the meatballs on the baking sheet after rolling them into 1-inch balls. **(3)** After 18 to 20 minutes in the oven, brush with olive oil and continue cooking until done. **(4)** Fill each bowl with meatballs, cucumber, feta, cherry tomatoes, and cauliflower rice. **(5)** Serve with lemon wedges, drizzled with tzatziki sauce, and garnished with fresh dill.

191. THAI ZOODLE CHICKEN SOUP

Total Time: 25 minutes | Prep Time: 10 minutes

Ingredients:

2 cups chicken broth	1 cup coconut milk (unsweetened)
1 chicken breast, cooked and shredded	1 cup zucchini noodles (zoodles)
1/2 cup mushrooms, sliced	1/2 red bell pepper, thinly sliced
1 teaspoon ginger, grated	2 cloves garlic, minced
1 tablespoon fish sauce	1 teaspoon red curry paste
Juice of 1 lime	1 tablespoon coconut oil
1/4 cup fresh cilantro, chopped	Salt and pepper to taste

Directions:

(1) Melt the coconut oil in a pot set over medium heat. Include the red curry paste, ginger, and garlic. Fry for a minute or two. **(2)** Add the coconut milk and chicken broth.

Reduce heat to low and stir well. **(3)** Before serving, garnish with chopped chicken, mushrooms, and bell pepper. Make sure to cook for at least 5 minutes. **(4)** Toss in the zucchini noodles, lime juice, fish sauce, and cilantro. For a further two minutes, reduce heat to low. **(5)** Add salt and pepper to taste. Take it off the stove and top it up with some chopped cilantro. Heat and serve immediately.

192. GRILLED TUNA STEAK WITH HERB BUTTER

Total Time: 15 minutes | Prep Time: 5 minutes

Ingredients:

2 tuna steaks (6 oz each)	2 tablespoons olive oil
1 teaspoon sea salt	1/2 teaspoon black pepper
1 teaspoon lemon zest	

For Herb Butter:

2 tablespoons unsalted butter, softened	1 tablespoon fresh parsley, chopped
1 teaspoon fresh thyme, chopped	1 garlic clove, minced
Juice of 1/2 lemon	

Directions:

(1) Get a grill or pan ready by heating it to medium-high. **(2)** Add olive oil, salt, pepper, and zest of a lemon to tuna steaks before grilling. **(3)** To achieve medium-rare doneness, grill for two to three minutes on each side or until done to your liking. **(4)** As the tuna cooks on the grill, combine the melted butter with the herbs and spices, garlic, and lemon juice. **(5)** After taking the tuna from the grill, brush it with herb butter and set it aside to rest for two minutes.

193. CAULIFLOWER RICE RISOTTO

Total Time: 20 minutes | Prep Time: 10 minutes

Ingredients:

2 cups cauliflower rice	1/2 cup heavy cream
1/4 cup grated Parmesan cheese	1/4 cup chicken or vegetable broth
1/2 cup mushrooms, chopped	1/4 cup onion, finely diced
2 cloves garlic, minced	1 tablespoon butter
1 tablespoon olive oil	Salt and pepper to taste
1 tablespoon fresh parsley, chopped	

Directions:

(1) In a skillet set over medium heat, melt the olive oil and butter. Get the onions and garlic soft by sautéing them. After 3 to 4 minutes, add the mushrooms and simmer until they are soft. **(2)** Coat the rice with cauliflower, then pour in the broth. After 5 minutes of cooking, stir periodically. **(3)** The heavy cream and Parmesan should be stirred in only before serving. After three more minutes of stirring, cook. **(4)** Add salt and pepper to taste. Warm and top with fresh parsley.

194. KETO CHOCOLATE CHIA PUDDING

Total Time: 2 hours 5 minutes (including chilling time) | Prep Time: 5 minutes

Ingredients:

1 cup unsweetened almond milk	2 tablespoons unsweetened cocoa powder
1/4 cup chia seeds	2 tablespoons erythritol or monk fruit sweetener

1/2 teaspoon vanilla extract
1/4 teaspoon sea salt
1/4 teaspoon cinnamon (optional)

Directions:

(1) Combine almond milk, cocoa powder, sweetener, cinnamon, sea salt, and vanilla, and stir in a bowl. *(2)* Before mixing, add the chia seeds. *(3)* Stir to avoid clumping after 5 minutes of sitting. *(4)* Keep in the fridge for a minimum of two hours, preferably all night. *(5)* After mixing, serve and enjoy!

195. GARLIC PARMESAN CHICKEN WINGS

Total Time: 40 minutes | Prep Time: 10 minutes | Cook Time: 30 minutes

Ingredients:

2 lbs chicken wings	2 tbsp olive oil
1 tsp salt	½ tsp black pepper
½ tsp garlic powder	½ tsp paprika
¼ cup unsalted butter, melted	3 cloves garlic, minced
⅓ cup grated Parmesan cheese	1 tbsp fresh parsley, chopped

Directions:

(1) Set oven temperature to 400°F. Sprinkle parchment paper on a baking pan. *(2)* Whisk together the paprika, olive oil, salt, black pepper, and garlic powder before adding the chicken wings to the bowl. *(3)* Bake the wings for 25-30 minutes, turning once halfway through, in a single layer on the baking sheet. *(4)* Combine the Parmesan cheese, minced garlic, and melted butter in another bowl. *(5)* Mix the garlic butter with the cooked wings and toss to coat. *(6)* While still hot, sprinkle with chopped parsley and serve.

196. ZOODLE CHICKEN STIR-FRY

Total Time: 25 minutes | Prep Time: 10 minutes | Cook Time: 15 minutes

Ingredients:

2 medium zucchinis, spiralized	1 lb boneless, skinless chicken breast, sliced
2 tbsp olive oil	3 cloves garlic, minced
1 red bell pepper, sliced	1 cup broccoli florets
2 tbsp soy sauce or coconut aminos	1 tsp sesame oil
½ tsp red pepper flakes (optional)	1 tbsp sesame seeds, for garnish

Directions:

(1) In a big skillet, heat one tablespoon of olive oil over medium-high heat. When the chicken is 6-7 minutes old, add it and continue cooking till it becomes golden brown. Lift out of the pan and place aside. *(2)* Toss in the broccoli, bell pepper, garlic, and leftover olive oil in the same skillet. Cook until softened, about three to 4 minutes. *(3)* Stir in the red pepper flakes, sesame oil, and soy sauce when you return the cooked chicken to the pan. *(4)* Toss in the zucchini noodles and continue cooking for another two minutes or until they are barely soft. *(5)* Take off the stove, top with sesame seeds, and serve right away.

197. LOW-CARB CHICKEN ALFREDO BAKE

Total Time: 40 minutes | Prep Time: 10 minutes | Cook Time: 30 minutes

Ingredients:

1 lb cooked chicken breast, shredded	2 cups cauliflower rice

1 cup heavy cream	½ cup grated Parmesan cheese
1 cup shredded mozzarella cheese	3 cloves garlic, minced
1 tsp Italian seasoning	½ tsp salt
¼ tsp black pepper	2 tbsp fresh parsley, chopped

Directions:

(1) Get your oven preheated to 375°F, which is 190°C. Butter or oil a baking dish. **(2)** Combine the shredded chicken, heavy cream, Cauliflower rice, Parmesan, mozzarella, garlic, Italian seasoning, salt, and black pepper in a bowl. **(3)** Spread the blend evenly in the baking dish after transferring it. **(4)** After 25 to 30 minutes in the oven, the mixture should be bubbling and brown. **(5)** Warm and top with fresh parsley.

198. CAULIFLOWER CRUST BREAKFAST PIZZA

Total Time: 35 minutes | Prep Time: 15 minutes | Cook Time: 20 minutes

Ingredients:

1 small head cauliflower, riced	1 egg
¼ cup grated Parmesan cheese	½ tsp garlic powder
½ tsp Italian seasoning	¼ tsp salt
¼ tsp black pepper	½ cup shredded mozzarella cheese
2 large eggs	4 strips of cooked bacon, crumbled
½ avocado, sliced	1 tbsp fresh chives, chopped

Directions:

(1) Set oven temperature to 400°F. Sprinkle parchment paper on a baking pan. **(2)** Add the egg, Parmesan, garlic powder, Italian seasoning, salt, and black pepper to the bowl of cauliflower rice. Stir to combine. **(3)** On the baking sheet, shape into a circular crust and bake for 12–15 minutes or until brown. **(4)** Scatter mozzarella cheese and break two eggs on top. Take it out of the oven and serve. **(5)** Bake for another 5 minutes or until the eggs are set. **(6)** Serve topped with avocado slices, crumbled bacon, and chives.

199. ASIAN CUCUMBER SALAD

Total Time: 10 minutes | Prep Time: 10 minutes

Ingredients:

2 large cucumbers, thinly sliced	2 tbsp rice vinegar
1 tbsp sesame oil	1 tbsp soy sauce (or coconut aminos for keto)
1 tsp erythritol or monk fruit sweetener	1 tsp grated ginger
1 clove garlic, minced	1 tsp sesame seeds
1 tbsp chopped green onions	1/4 tsp red pepper flakes (optional)

Directions:

(1) Whisk together the sesame oil, rice vinegar, ginger, garlic, soy sauce, and sweetener in a bowl. **(2)** Toss in the sliced cucumbers so they are uniformly coated. **(3)** Toss on some sesame seeds, green onions, or red pepper flakes for a tasty garnish. **(4)** Give it 5 minutes to settle so the flavors can combine. Enjoy chilled.

200. KETO STUFFED BELL PEPPERS

Total Time: 40 minutes | Prep Time: 10 minutes | Cook Time: 30 minutes

Ingredients:

4 bell peppers (any color), halved and deseeded	1 lb ground turkey or beef
1/2 cup cauliflower rice	1/2 cup diced tomatoes (no sugar added)
1/2 cup shredded mozzarella cheese	1/4 cup chopped onions
2 cloves garlic, minced	1 tsp Italian seasoning
1/2 tsp salt	1/4 tsp black pepper
1 tbsp olive oil	

Directions:

(1) Get your oven preheated to 375°F, which is 190°C. *(2)* To get the best results, warm the olive oil in a skillet over medium heat. After 2 minutes of sautéing, add garlic and onions. *(3)* Toss in the ground beef or turkey and brown it. Get rid of any extra fat. *(4)* Add the parboiled rice, chopped tomatoes, Italian seasoning, salt, and pepper, and mix well. Low heat for five minutes. *(5)* After stuffing the bell pepper halves, sprinkle with shredded cheese. *(6)* Once baked for 25 minutes, the peppers and cheese should be tender and melted. Heat and serve immediately.

201. LOW-CARB CABBAGE STIR-FRY

Total Time: 20 minutes | Prep Time: 10 minutes | Cook Time: 10 minutes

Ingredients:

4 cups shredded cabbage	1/2 lb ground chicken or beef
1/2 cup sliced bell peppers	1/4 cup chopped onions
2 cloves garlic, minced	1 tbsp coconut oil
2 tbsp soy sauce (or coconut aminos)	1 tsp grated ginger
1/2 tsp red pepper flakes (optional)	1 tsp sesame seeds

Directions:

(1) Melt the coconut oil in a pot set over medium heat. *(2)* Saute the onions, ginger, and garlic. Cook for another minute. *(3)* Before browning, add ground meat (chicken or beef). *(4)* Add the bell peppers, cabbage, soy sauce, and red pepper flakes and stir to combine. To soften the cabbage, cook for around seven to seven minutes. *(5)* Before serving, top with sesame seeds.

202. CREAMY SPINACH STUFFED MUSHROOMS

Total Time: 25 minutes | Prep Time: 10 minutes | Cook Time: 15 minutes

Ingredients:

8 large mushrooms, stems removed	1 cup fresh spinach, chopped
1/2 cup cream cheese, softened	1/4 cup shredded Parmesan cheese
1 clove garlic, minced	1/2 tsp salt
1/4 tsp black pepper	1 tbsp olive oil

Directions:

(1) Get your oven preheated to 375°F, which is 190°C. *(2)* To get the best results, warm the olive oil in a skillet over medium heat. Toss in the garlic and sauté for 2 minutes or until the spinach wilts. *(3)* Add the cream cheese, Parmesan, salt, and pepper to the sautéed spinach. *(4)* Before placing them in a baking pan, stuff mushrooms with the mixture. *(5)* After the mixture has bubbled and the mushrooms have softened, bake for another 15 minutes. *(6)* Keep heated before serving.

203. ASIAN SESAME CHICKEN LETTUCE WRAPS

Total Time: 25 minutes | Prep Time: 15 minutes | Cook Time: 10 minutes

Ingredients:

- 1 lb ground chicken
- 1-inch piece ginger, grated
- 1 tbsp sesame oil
- 1 tbsp hoisin sauce (optional)
- 1/4 cup green onions, chopped
- 1/4 cup water chestnuts, chopped
- Butter lettuce leaves
- 2 cloves garlic, minced
- 1/4 cup low-sodium soy sauce
- 1 tbsp rice vinegar
- 1 tsp sriracha (optional, for heat)
- 1/4 cup shredded carrots
- 1 tbsp sesame seeds

Directions:

(1) ConductConduct a large skillet at a medium-high temperature. Toss in the sesame oil and cook the ginger and garlic for a minute or two. **(2)** Brown the ground chicken by adding it and breaking it apart while it cooks. **(3)** Blend in the sriracha, hoisin sauce, rice vinegar, and soy sauce. Add three to four more minutes of cooking time. **(4)** Toss in some water chestnuts, green onions, and carrots. Combine together and continue cooking for an additional minute. **(5)** Before topping with sesame seeds, take off the heat. **(6)** Garnish the mixture with butter lettuce leaves and serve.

204. SPAGHETTI SQUASH PUTTANESCA

Total Time: 40 minutes | Prep Time: 10 minutes | Cook Time: 30 minutes

Ingredients:

- 1 medium spaghetti squash, halved and seeded
- 2 cloves garlic, minced
- 1/4 cup black olives, sliced
- 1/2 tsp red pepper flakes
- 1/4 cup fresh parsley, chopped
- Salt and pepper to taste
- 2 tbsp olive oil, divided
- 1/2 cup cherry tomatoes, halved
- 1 tbsp capers
- 1/2 tsp dried oregano
- 1/4 cup grated Parmesan (optional)

Directions:

(1) Set oven temperature to 400°F. Half of the spaghetti squash, cut side down, should be brushed with one tablespoon of olive oil before placing on a baking pan. To make the soft meat, roast it for half an hour. **(2)** The first step is to add the olive oil—about a tablespoon's worth—to a skillet and heat it over medium heat. Simmer for 30 seconds after adding garlic. **(3)** Cherry tomatoes, olives, capers, red pepper flakes, and oregano should all be mixed together. To make the tomatoes softer, cook for 5 minutes. **(4)** Before adding the spaghetti squash strands to the pan, scrape them out with a fork. Mix by tossing. **(5)** Take it off the stove, add some pepper and salt, then top it all up with some Parmesan and fresh parsley.

205. BAKED PARMESAN EGGPLANT SLICES

Total Time: 30 minutes | Prep Time: 10 minutes | Cook Time: 20 minutes

Ingredients:

- 1 medium eggplant, sliced into 1/4-inch rounds
- 1/2 cup grated Parmesan cheese
- 1/2 tsp dried oregano
- 1/4 tsp salt
- 1 tbsp olive oil
- 1/2 tsp garlic powder
- 1/4 tsp black pepper

Directions:

(1) Set oven temperature to 400°F. Sprinkle parchment paper on a baking pan. **(2)** Drizzle a little olive oil over each side of the eggplant pieces. **(3)** Chop the oregano, Parmesan, garlic powder, black pepper, and salt and combine in a small bowl. **(4)** Coat both sides of each eggplant slice by pressing it into the Parmesan mixture. *(5)* Put the slices on a baking pan and bake, turning once, for 20 minutes. *(6)* Warm & enjoy as a snack or side dish.

206. CAPRESE SALAD WITH BALSAMIC GLAZE

Total Time: 10 minutes | Prep Time: 10 minutes

Ingredients:

- 2 large tomatoes, sliced
- 1/4 cup fresh basil leaves
- 2 tbsp balsamic glaze
- 1/4 tsp black pepper
- 8 oz fresh mozzarella, sliced
- 2 tbsp extra virgin olive oil
- 1/4 tsp salt

Directions:

(1) On a serving platter, alternate the slices of tomato and mozzarella. *(2)* Put a few sprigs of fresh basil in between each slice. *(3)* Balsamic glaze and olive oil should be drizzled over. *(4)* Add salt and pepper to taste. Make sure to serve right away.

207. LOW-CARB FRENCH ONION SOUP

Total Time: 1 hour 10 minutes | Prep Time: 10 minutes | Cook Time: 1 hour

Ingredients:

- 2 large onions, thinly sliced
- 2 cloves garlic, minced
- 1/2 cup dry white wine (optional)
- 1/2 tsp thyme
- 1/2 cup shredded Gruyère cheese
- 4 slices of keto-friendly bread (or almond flour bread)
- 3 tbsp butter
- 4 cups beef broth (low sodium)
- 1 tsp Worcestershire sauce
- Salt and pepper to taste
- 1/2 cup shredded mozzarella cheese

Directions:

(1) In a tall saucepan set over medium heat, melt the butter. After 30–40 minutes of cooking, add the sliced onions and stir periodically to caramelize. *(2)* Cook for an additional minute after adding minced garlic. *(3)* Simmer for five minutes to reduce, then add white wine if using. *(4)* Stock, Worcestershire sauce, thyme, pepper, salt, and beef broth should be added. Reduce heat to low & continue cooking for 15 more minutes. *(5)* Set oven temperature to 375°F. *(6)* Spoon the soup into dishes that can be baked. Toss some shredded cheese over each dish and top with a keto bread piece. *(7)* To get melted and golden cheese, broil for three to five minutes. *(8)* Enjoy while hot!

208. CREAMY SPINACH ARTICHOKE DIP

Total Time: 30 minutes | Prep Time: 10 minutes | Cook Time: 20 minutes

Ingredients:

- 1 cup fresh spinach, chopped
- 4 oz cream cheese, softened
- 1/4 cup mayonnaise
- 1/4 cup grated Parmesan cheese
- 1/2 tsp onion powder
- 1/2 cup canned artichoke hearts, drained
- 1/2 cup sour cream
- 1/2 cup shredded mozzarella cheese
- 2 cloves garlic, minced
- Salt and pepper to taste

Directions:

(1) Get your oven preheated to 375°F, which is 190°C. *(2)* Be sure to thoroughly blend the cream cheese, sour cream, and mayonnaise in a mixing dish. *(3)* Before serving, toss in the spinach, artichoke hearts, garlic powder, salt,

and pepper. *(4)* Combine with the Parmesan and mozzarella cheeses. *(5)* Evenly distribute the ingredients in a small baking dish. *(6)* To get a golden and bubbly top, bake for 20 minutes. *(7)* Warmed and accompanied with keto-friendly crackers or crisp vegetables, serve.

209. ROASTED CAULIFLOWER TABBOULEH

Total Time: 30 minutes | Prep Time: 10 minutes | Cook Time: 20 minutes

Ingredients:

1 small head of cauliflower, grated	1/2 cup cherry tomatoes, diced
1/2 cucumber, diced	1/4 cup red onion, finely chopped
1/4 cup fresh parsley, chopped	2 tbsp fresh mint, chopped
3 tbsp olive oil	2 tbsp lemon juice
1 tsp garlic powder	Salt and pepper to taste

Directions:

(1) Set oven temperature to 400°F. *(2)* In a baking dish, distribute the cauliflower rice evenly and pour in the olive oil, measuring out one tablespoon. Prepare, stirring once or twice, for 15 to 20 minutes or until a little brown. Allow to cool. *(3)* After the cauliflower has roasted, place it in a bowl with the cucumber, parsley, mint, cherry tomatoes, and red onion. Top with the remaining lemon juice and olive oil. *(4)* Season with salt & pepper, then stir in garlic powder. *(5)* Enjoy as a refreshing side dish, either cold or served at room temperature.

210. SPAGHETTI SQUASH WITH PESTO

Total Time: 45 minutes | Prep Time: 10 minutes | Cook Time: 35 minutes

Ingredients:

1 medium spaghetti squash	2 tbsp olive oil
1/2 cup basil pesto (homemade or store-bought, keto-friendly)	1/4 cup grated Parmesan cheese
1/2 tsp garlic powder	Salt and pepper to taste
1/4 tsp red pepper flakes (optional)	

Directions:

(1) Set oven temperature to 400°F. *(2)* After halving the spaghetti squash lengthwise, remove its seeds. Before seasoning with salt and pepper, brush the inside with olive oil. *(3)* Roast, with the cut side down, for 30–35 minutes or until soft. *(4)* After it has cooled a little, scoop out the spaghetti-like strands into a basin using a fork. *(5)* Garlic powder, Parmesan cheese, pesto, and red pepper flakes (if used) should be mixed with the spaghetti squash. *(6)* This low-carb pasta substitute is wonderful when served warm.

211. CREAMY GARLIC HERB DIP

Total Time: 10 minutes | Prep Time: 10 minutes

Ingredients:

1 cup Greek yogurt (plain, unsweetened)	2 tbsp olive oil
2 cloves garlic, minced	1 tbsp fresh parsley, chopped
1 tbsp fresh dill, chopped	1 tbsp fresh chives, chopped
1 tsp lemon juice	½ tsp sea salt
¼ tsp black pepper	

Directions:

(1) Whisk together the olive oil and Greek yogurt in a large bowl. *(2)* Include chopped dill, parsley, chives, and minced garlic. *(3)* Mix in the pepper, salt, and lemon juice. *(4)* Stir until combined and creamy. *(5)* Top grilled meats with this, or serve with fresh vegetables.

212. HERB-CRUSTED WHITEFISH

Total Time: 20 minutes | Prep Time: 5 minutes | Cook Time: 15 minutes

Ingredients:

2 whitefish fillets (such as cod or tilapia)	2 tbsp olive oil
¼ cup almond flour	1 tbsp fresh parsley, chopped
1 tsp dried thyme	1 tsp dried oregano
½ tsp garlic powder	½ tsp sea salt
¼ tsp black pepper	1 lemon, cut into wedges

Directions:

(1) Set oven temperature to 400°F. Sprinkle parchment paper on a baking pan. *(2)* Parsley, thyme, oregano, almond flour, garlic powder, salt, and pepper should be combined in a small basin. *(3)* Before coating the whitefish fillets uniformly with the herb mixture, brush them with olive oil. *(4)* After 12–15 minutes in the oven, or when the fish flakes easily, transfer to a baking sheet. *(5)* Cut into wedges and serve.

213. ROASTED VEGGIE AND SHRIMP SKILLET

Total Time: 25 minutes | Prep Time: 10 minutes | Cook Time: 15 minutes

Ingredients:

1 lb shrimp, peeled and deveined	1 zucchini, sliced
1 red bell pepper, chopped	1 cup cherry tomatoes, halved
½ red onion, sliced	2 tbsp olive oil
1 tsp smoked paprika	½ tsp garlic powder
½ tsp sea salt	¼ tsp black pepper
½ tsp dried oregano	½ lemon, juiced

Directions:

(1) In a big skillet, heat up one tablespoon of olive oil over medium heat. *(2)* Combine with the red onion, cherry tomatoes, bell pepper, and zucchini. Add the garlic and sauté for around seven to eight minutes. *(3)* Combine the smoked paprika, garlic powder, shrimp, and the rest of the olive oil in a bowl. Season with salt and pepper. *(4)* Sauté the shrimp for three to four minutes on each side or until they become pink and are opaque throughout. *(5)* Toss in the dried oregano and top with a squeeze of fresh lemon juice. Keep heated before serving.

214. LEMON THYME GRILLED VEGETABLES

Total Time: 20 minutes | Prep Time: 10 minutes | Cook Time: 10 minutes

Ingredients:

1 zucchini, sliced	1 yellow squash, sliced
1 red bell pepper, chopped	½ red onion, sliced
2 tbsp olive oil	1 tsp fresh thyme, chopped
½ tsp garlic powder	½ tsp sea salt
¼ tsp black pepper	½ lemon, juiced

Directions:

(1) Warm up the grill to a medium-high temperature. *(2)* Toss the onion, bell pepper, zucchini, and squash with the olive oil, thyme, garlic powder, salt, and pepper in a large

bowl. **(3)** Grill the veggies for three to four minutes on each side or until they are soft and slightly blackened. **(4)** Once grilled, take off the heat and add a little lemon juice. Keep heated before serving.

215. AVOCADO BACON CHICKEN SALAD

Total Time: 20 minutes | Prep Time: 15 minutes

Ingredients:

2 cups cooked chicken breast, shredded	1 large avocado, diced
4 slices turkey bacon, cooked and crumbled	1/4 cup red onion, diced
1/4 cup cherry tomatoes, halved	2 tablespoons mayonnaise (or Greek yogurt)
1 teaspoon Dijon mustard	1 teaspoon lemon juice
Salt and pepper to taste	1/4 teaspoon garlic powder
2 cups mixed greens	

Directions:

(1) Add the chopped avocado, crumbled bacon, red onion, cherry tomatoes, and shredded chicken to a big bowl. **(2)** Combine the mayonnaise (or Greek yogurt), Dijon mustard, lemon juice, garlic powder, salt, & pepper in a small receptacle. **(3)** Toss the chicken mixture slightly to coat it with the dressing. **(4)** Top with a variety of greens and savor.

216. CAULIFLOWER PIZZA WITH PESTO

Total Time: 40 minutes | Prep Time: 15 minutes

Ingredients:

For the Crust:

1 small head of cauliflower, riced	1/2 cup shredded mozzarella cheese
1/4 cup grated Parmesan cheese	1 egg, beaten
1/2 teaspoon garlic powder	1/2 teaspoon dried oregano
Salt and pepper to taste	

For the Toppings:

1/4 cup pesto sauce	1/2 cup shredded mozzarella cheese
1/4 cup cherry tomatoes, halved	1/4 cup black olives, sliced
1/4 teaspoon red pepper flakes (optional)	Fresh basil leaves for garnish

Directions:

(1) Roll out parchment paper and set the oven temperature to 400 degrees Fahrenheit. **(2)** Cook the riced cauliflower in a microwave-safe dish for 5 minutes until tender, then set aside to cool. After that, wrap it in a dry towel and press down any extra moisture. **(3)** Combine the chopped cauliflower with the Parmesan, mozzarella, egg, garlic powder, oregano, salt, and pepper in a mixer bowl. **(4)** Form a thin crust by pressing the mixture onto the baking sheet. Just a few more minutes in the oven should do the trick to get that golden color. **(5)** Once the crust is coated with pesto sauce, add mozzarella, tomatoes, and olives on top. **(6)** To melt the cheese, bake for an additional 10 minutes. **(7)** Some red pepper flakes and basil leaves make a nice garnish. Keep heated before serving.

217. MEDITERRANEAN ZOODLE SALAD

Total Time: 15 minutes | Prep Time: 10 minutes

Ingredients:

2 medium zucchinis, spiralized	1/4 cup cherry tomatoes, halved
1/4 cup cucumber, diced	1/4 cup red bell pepper, diced
1/4 cup Kalamata olives, sliced	2 tablespoons crumbled feta cheese
1 tablespoon olive oil	1 tablespoon lemon juice
1/2 teaspoon dried oregano	Salt and pepper to taste

Directions:

(1) In a large basin, combine squash spirals, cherry tomatoes, cucumber, red bell pepper, olives, and feta cheese. Shake to combine. *(2)* Whisk together the oregano, lemon juice, olive oil, salt, and pepper in a small bowl. *(3)* Toss the salad lightly to coat it with the dressing. *(4)* Put it in the fridge for 10 minutes to let the flavors combine, or serve it right away.

218. PESTO ZOODLE BOWL

Total Time: 15 minutes | Prep Time: 10 minutes

Ingredients:

2 medium zucchinis, spiralized	1/2 cup cherry tomatoes, halved
1/4 cup pesto sauce	1/4 cup shredded Parmesan cheese
1/4 teaspoon red pepper flakes (optional	1 tablespoon olive oil
1/4 teaspoon garlic powder	Salt and pepper to taste
1/4 cup toasted pine nuts (optional)	

Directions:

(1) Grease a pan and place it on a medium heat setting. While cooking, sauté the spiralized zucchini for 2 minutes. *(2)* Warm through, then stir in garlic powder, pesto sauce, salt, and pepper. Cook for an additional 2 minutes. *(3)* Take it off the stove and stir in the cherry tomatoes. *(4)* Sprinkle some toasted pine nuts, red pepper flakes, and Parmesan on top. *(5)* Make sure to serve right away.

219. BROCCOLI SLAW STIR-FRY

Total Time: 15 minutes | Prep Time: 5 minutes

Ingredients:

1 tbsp olive oil	2 cloves garlic, minced
1 tsp fresh ginger, minced	1 (12 oz) bag of broccoli slaw
1/2 red bell pepper, thinly sliced	1/2 cup snap peas, trimmed
2 tbsp coconut aminos	1 tsp sesame oil
1/2 tsp red pepper flakes (optional)	2 tbsp chopped green onions
1 tbsp sesame seeds	

Directions:

(1) Spread out the olive oil and set it over medium heat in a large pan. After 30 seconds, add the ginger and garlic and cook until they smell good. *(2)* Toss in the snap peas, bell pepper, and broccoli slaw. Add the ingredients and stir-fry for around four to five minutes. *(3)* Mix in the sesame oil, red pepper flakes, and coconut aminos. Be sure to mix well. *(4)* After the first 3 minutes, cook for a further three until the vegetables are soft but still not mushy. *(5)* Sesame seeds and green onions make a beautiful garnish. Keep heated before serving.

220. ZOODLE STIR-FRY WITH TOFU

Total Time: 20 minutes | Prep Time: 10 minutes

Ingredients:

- 1 block (14 oz) firm tofu, drained and cubed
- 1 tbsp avocado oil
- 1/2 tsp salt
- 2 medium zucchinis, spiralized
- 1/2 cup mushrooms, sliced
- 1/2 red bell pepper, thinly sliced
- 1 tbsp coconut aminos
- 1 tsp rice vinegar
- 1/2 tsp garlic powder
- 1/2 tsp red pepper flakes (optional
- 1 tbsp chopped cilantro

Directions:

(1) Put the avocado oil in a skillet and set it over medium-high heat. For around five to seven minutes, or until the tofu pieces become brown, toss periodically while cooking. Season with salt. Detach and put aside. **(2)** Sauté the bell pepper and mushrooms for three minutes in the same pan. **(3)** Gather the zoodles, rice vinegar, coconut aminos, garlic powder, and red pepper flakes. Sauté for a further two minutes. **(4)** Put the tofu back in the pan, mix everything well, and let it simmer for one more minute. **(5)** Serve right away with a sprinkle of chopped cilantro.

221. CHEESY ZUCCHINI CASSEROLE

Total Time: 35 minutes | Prep Time: 10 minutes

Ingredients:

- 3 medium zucchinis, thinly sliced
- 1/2 tsp salt
- 1/2 cup cottage cheese
- 1/2 cup shredded mozzarella cheese
- 2 tbsp Parmesan cheese
- 1 large egg
- 1/2 tsp garlic powder
- 1/2 tsp dried oregano
- 1/4 tsp black pepper

Directions:

(1) Heat the oven to 375 degrees Fahrenheit. Pat a baking dish dry. **(2)** Slice the zucchini, add the salt, and set aside for 10 minutes in a colander. Pat dry. **(3)** A bowl should be used to beat the cottage cheese, mozzarella, Parmesan, egg, garlic powder, oregano, and black pepper. Arrange the sliced zucchini in the baking dish and top with the cheese mixture. **(4)** Put the cheese on top and repeat layering until you've used all the ingredients. **(5)** To get a golden color and a frothy top, bake for 25 minutes. Serve after a little cooling period.

222. CAULIFLOWER "RISOTTO" WITH MUSHROOMS

Total Time: 20 minutes | Prep Time: 10 minutes

Ingredients:

- 1 tbsp olive oil
- 1/2 cup onion, finely chopped
- 2 cloves garlic, minced
- 1 1/2 cups mushrooms, sliced
- 3 cups riced cauliflower
- 1/2 cup unsweetened almond milk
- 1/2 cup grated Parmesan cheese
- 1/2 tsp salt
- 1/4 tsp black pepper
- 1/4 tsp dried thyme

Directions:

(1) To get the best results, warm the olive oil in a skillet over medium heat. Cook the garlic and onion for two minutes. **(2)** Sauté the mushrooms for 5 minutes or until they soften.

(3) Before serving, mix in the almond milk, Parmesan, cauliflower rice, salt, pepper, and thyme. **(4)** Stir often and cook for 5 to 7 minutes or until soft and creamy. **(5)** If preferred, serve warm with an additional sprinkle of Parmesan.

223. GREEK CHICKEN GYRO BOWLS

Total Time: 40 minutes | Prep Time: 15 minutes

Ingredients:

2 boneless, skinless chicken breasts	2 tbsp olive oil
1 tbsp lemon juice	2 cloves garlic, minced
1 tsp dried oregano	½ tsp cumin
½ tsp salt	¼ tsp black pepper
1 cup quinoa, cooked	1 cup cherry tomatoes, halved
1 small cucumber, diced	¼ red onion, thinly sliced
½ cup crumbled feta cheese	¼ cup kalamata olives, sliced
¼ cup tzatziki sauce	1 tbsp fresh parsley, chopped

Directions:

(1) Combine the olive oil, tangerine juice, garlic, cumin, oregano, salt, and pepper in a bowl. After 15 minutes of marinating, add the chicken strips. **(2)** Fry the chicken for six to eight minutes on each side in a pan heated over medium heat or until brown and cooked through. **(3)** Serve the cooked quinoa in individual bowls. **(4)** Pile atop the grilled chicken, sliced cucumber, feta, olives, and cherry tomatoes. **(5)** Prior to serving, top with tzatziki sauce and garnish with fresh parsley.

224. CREAMY TUSCAN SALMON

Total Time: 30 minutes | Prep Time: 10 minutes

Ingredients:

2 salmon fillets	1 tbsp olive oil
½ tsp salt	¼ tsp black pepper
2 cloves garlic, minced	½ cup cherry tomatoes, halved
1 cup baby spinach	½ cup coconut milk
¼ cup grated Parmesan cheese	1 tsp Italian seasoning
½ tsp red pepper flakes (optional)	

Directions:

(1) Dress the salmon fillets with pepper and salt. **(2)** Grease a pan and place it on a medium heat setting. Before flipping the fish, cook it for another four or five minutes in a pan over medium heat. Detach and put aside. **(3)** While the garlic is softening, sauté the cherry tomatoes in the same pan. **(4)** When the young spinach wilts, add it to the pan. **(5)** Red pepper flakes, Italian spice, Parmesan cheese, and coconut milk should be added. Be sure to mix well. **(6)** After 5 minutes of simmering, add the salmon back to the pan with the sauce. **(7)** Warm it up and serve it over cauliflower rice or steamed veggies.

225. CUCUMBER DILL YOGURT SALAD

Total Time: 15 minutes | Prep Time: 10 minutes

Ingredients:

2 cucumbers, thinly sliced	½ cup Greek yogurt
1 tbsp lemon juice	1 tbsp fresh dill, chopped
1 small garlic clove, minced	½ tsp salt
¼ tsp black pepper	

Directions:

(1) Combine the dill, garlic, lemon juice, Greek yogurt, salt, and pepper in a bowl. *(2)* Toss in the cucumber slices so they are covered evenly. *(3)* Before serving, let it rest for 5 minutes so flavors may infuse. *(4)* For a cool and refreshing side dish, serve chilled.

226. CHICKEN ZOODLE PHO

Total Time: 35 minutes | Prep Time: 15 minutes

Ingredients:

2 cups low-sodium chicken broth	1 tbsp coconut aminos (or soy sauce alternative)
1-inch piece ginger, sliced	1 clove garlic, minced
½ tsp ground coriander	½ tsp ground cinnamon
1 boneless, skinless chicken breast	1 small zucchini, spiralized into noodles
½ cup bean sprouts	2 green onions, sliced
¼ cup fresh cilantro, chopped	½ lime, sliced into wedges

Directions:

(1) Get the coconut aminos, chicken broth, ginger, garlic, cilantro, and cinnamon going in a saucepan. Heat till simmering. *(2)* Before the chicken is done cooking, add the breasts and simmer for another 12 to 15 minutes. Cut off and discard. *(3)* Spoon the zucchini noodles into the dishes to be served. *(4)* Add shredded chicken, bean sprouts, and green onions to the noodles after pouring heated broth over them. *(5)* Lime wedges and fresh cilantro make a lovely garnish.

227. CUCUMBER MINT YOGURT SALAD

Total Time: 10 minutes | Prep Time: 10 minutes

Ingredients:

1 large cucumber, thinly sliced	1 cup Greek yogurt (unsweetened)
1 tbsp fresh mint, chopped	1 tbsp lemon juice
½ tsp salt	¼ tsp black pepper
1 garlic clove, minced (optional)	

Directions:

(1) Toss the melted garlic with the Greek yogurt, lemon juice, salt, and pepper after it has cooled somewhat. Mix well. *(2)* Toss the cucumber slices and mint leaves into the mixing basin. *(3)* Combine the ingredients and toss the cucumbers so that they are covered equally with the yogurt dressing. *(4)* Put it in the fridge for 10 minutes to cool before serving, or serve it right away.

228. CHICKEN AND BROCCOLI ALFREDO BAKE

Total Time: 40 minutes | Prep Time: 10 minutes

Ingredients:

2 boneless, skinless chicken breasts, diced	2 cups broccoli florets
1 cup cauliflower rice	1 cup unsweetened almond milk
½ cup Parmesan cheese, grated	2 tbsp cream cheese
1 tsp garlic powder	½ tsp salt
¼ tsp black pepper	1 tbsp olive oil

Directions:

(1) Set oven temperature to 375°F. Apply olive oil to a baking dish. *(2)* Saute the chicken cubes in olive oil in a skillet over medium heat

for about five to seven minutes or until done. *(3)* After three or four minutes of steaming, the broccoli should be just slightly soft. *(4)* Add the almond milk, garlic powder, salt, pepper, cream cheese, and Parmesan cheese to a pot and stir until melted. Blend well. *(5)* Put the cauliflower rice, cooked chicken, and broccoli in the prepared baking dish in layers. After that, dollop the Alfredo sauce all over. *(6)* To get a golden crust and bubbling center, bake for 20 minutes. *(7)* Enjoy while hot!

229. HERB-CRUSTED PORK CHOPS

Total Time: 25 minutes | Prep Time: 10 minutes

Ingredients:

2 boneless pork chops	1 tbsp olive oil
½ cup almond flour	1 tsp dried thyme
1 tsp dried rosemary	½ tsp garlic powder
½ tsp salt	¼ tsp black pepper

Directions:

(1) Get your oven preheated to 375°F, which is 190°C. Sprinkle parchment paper on a baking pan. *(2)* Combine almond flour, ground garlic, rosemary, thyme, salt, and pepper in a small basin. *(3)* Coat the pork chops equally with the herb mixture after brushing them with olive oil. *(4)* Let the pork chops rest for 15 to 18 minutes after taking them out of the oven until their internal heat reaches 145°F. *(5)* After 5 minutes, set aside to cool.

230. HERB-CRUSTED GRILLED SALMON

Total Time: 20 minutes | Prep Time: 10 minutes

Ingredients:

2 salmon fillets	1 tbsp olive oil
1 tbsp Dijon mustard	½ cup almond flour
1 tsp dried dill	1 tsp dried parsley
½ tsp garlic powder	½ tsp salt
¼ tsp black pepper	

Directions:

(1) Grill until it is medium-hot. *(2)* Toss together almond flour, parsley, dill, garlic powder, pepper, and salt in a bowl. *(3)* Apply a combination of olive oil and Dijon mustard to the salmon fillets, then sprinkle over the herb mixture. *(4)* Seafood should be grilled for four to five minutes on each side or until it flakes readily when tested with a fork. *(5)* Warm it up and serve it with some steamed veggies or a green salad.

231. SPAGHETTI SQUASH CARBONARA

Total Time: 40 minutes | Prep Time: 10 minutes | Cook Time: 30 minutes

Ingredients:

1 medium spaghetti squash	2 slices turkey bacon, chopped
2 cloves garlic, minced	2 large eggs
¼ cup grated Parmesan cheese	¼ teaspoon salt
¼ teaspoon black pepper	1 tablespoon olive oil
2 tablespoons chopped parsley	

Directions:

(1) Set oven temperature to 400°F. After halves the spaghetti squash, scoop out its seeds and set halves cut-side down on a baking pan. Bake for half an hour or until soft. *(2)* Get the turkey bacon crispy by cooking it in a skillet over medium heat. After one minute, add the garlic. Take it out of the oven. *(3)* Combine the eggs, Parmesan, salt, and pepper in a mixing bowl. *(4)* Toss in the bacon and

spaghetti squash after scraping it into strands with a fork. **(5)** Toss the squash to coat it with sauce, then quickly stir in the egg mixture. **(6)** Top with chopped parsley, drizzle with olive oil and serve hot.

232. CHILI LIME GRILLED SHRIMP

Total Time: 20 minutes | Prep Time: 10 minutes | Cook Time: 10 minutes

Ingredients:

1 lb large shrimp, peeled and deveined	2 tablespoons olive oil
Juice of 1 lime	1 teaspoon lime zest
1 teaspoon chili powder	½ teaspoon garlic powder
½ teaspoon cumin	¼ teaspoon salt
¼ teaspoon black pepper	2 tablespoons chopped cilantro

Directions:

(1) Combine olive oil, lime zest, lime juice, garlic powder, cumin, salt, & black pepper in a bowl. Add chili powder and garlic powder. **(2)** Coat the shrimp by tossing them in the marinade. Ten minutes is all it takes. **(3)** Bring a grill or pan to a medium-high temperature. **(4)** Grill the shrimp either on skewers or in a pan. Cook for two to three minutes on each side or until opaque and done. **(5)** After taking it off the grill, garnish it with cilantro and serve it right away.

233. CILANTRO LIME CAULIFLOWER RICE

Total Time: 15 minutes | Prep Time: 5 minutes | Cook Time: 10 minutes

Ingredients:

1 head cauliflower, riced	1 tablespoon olive oil
Juice of 1 lime	1 teaspoon lime zest
½ teaspoon garlic powder	¼ teaspoon salt
¼ teaspoon black pepper	2 tablespoons chopped cilantro

Directions:

(1) Prepare the olive oil for optimal results by warming it in a pan set over medium heat. Incorporate the cauliflower rice and sauté, stirring often, for five to 7 minutes or until soft. **(2)** Add the lime zest, lime juice, garlic powder, salt, and black pepper, and thoroughly mix. **(3)** Stir in the chopped cilantro after taking off the heat. **(4)** Use it as a carb-light accompaniment or a foundation for your favorite dishes.

234. TURKEY ZUCCHINI MEATBALLS

Total Time: 35 minutes | Prep Time: 10 minutes | Cook Time: 25 minutes

Ingredients:

1 lb ground turkey	1 small zucchini, grated
1 egg	¼ cup almond flour
2 cloves garlic, minced	½ teaspoon onion powder
½ teaspoon salt	¼ teaspoon black pepper
1 teaspoon Italian seasoning	1 tablespoon olive oil

Directions:

(1) Get your oven preheated to 375°F, which is 190°C. Sprinkle parchment paper on a baking pan. **(2)** Combine the chicken, zucchini, egg, almond flour, garlic powder, onion powder, salt, pepper, and Italian seasoning in a bowl. **(3)** Roll the dough into meatballs that are one inch in diameter and set them on a baking pan. **(4)** Before serving, brush the meatballs with olive oil. **(5)** To get a golden brown color and ensure doneness, bake for 25 minutes. *(6)* Top with cauliflower rice or a low-carb sauce, and serve.

235. CHEESY SPINACH AND EGG BAKE

Total Time: 40 minutes | Prep Time: 10 minutes

Ingredients:

- 6 large eggs
- ½ cup shredded cheddar cheese
- ¼ cup heavy cream
- ½ teaspoon salt
- 1 tablespoon olive oil
- 1 cup fresh spinach, chopped
- ¼ cup feta cheese, crumbled
- 1 teaspoon garlic powder
- ¼ teaspoon black pepper

Directions:

(1) Get your oven preheated to 375°F, which is 190°C. Melt the olive oil in an 8-by-8-inch baking dish. *(2)* Mash the eggs with the heavy cream, garlic powder, salt, and pepper in a bowl. *(3)* Combine spinach, feta, and cheddar cheese. *(4)* Transfer the blend to the baking dish that has been preheated. *(5)* Set the center by baking for 25 to 30 minutes. *(6)* After letting it cool for a while, slice it. Keep heated before serving.

236. AVOCADO EGG SALAD LETTUCE WRAPS

Total Time: 15 minutes | Prep Time: 10 minutes

Ingredients:

- 3 hard-boiled eggs, chopped
- 1 tablespoon mayonnaise
- 1 ripe avocado, mashed
- ½ teaspoon Dijon mustard
- ½ teaspoon lemon juice
- ¼ teaspoon salt
- ¼ teaspoon garlic powder
- ⅛ teaspoon black pepper
- 4 large lettuce leaves (romaine or butter lettuce)

Directions:

(1) In a bowl, combine the avocado, eggs, sauce, Dijon mustard, lemon juice, garlic powder, salt, and pepper. Add the lemon juice and combine well. *(2)* Blend well by stirring. *(3)* Using a spoon, top each lettuce leaf with the egg salad. *(4)* Serve right away by encasing the filling in lettuce.

237. KETO ZUCCHINI BREAD

Total Time: 55 minutes | Prep Time: 15 minutes

Ingredients:

- 1½ cups almond flour
- ½ teaspoon cinnamon
- 2 large eggs
- ¼ cup coconut oil, melted
- ½ cup shredded zucchini (squeeze out excess moisture)
- ½ teaspoon baking soda
- ¼ teaspoon salt
- ¼ cup unsweetened almond mil
- 1 teaspoon vanilla extract
- ¼ cup sugar-free sweetener

Directions:

(1) Preheating the oven to 350°F is the recommended option. Apply some oil to a loaf pan that measures nine by 5 inches. *(2)* Combine the almond flour, baking soda, cinnamon, and salt in a mixing dish. *(3)* Melt the coconut oil & stir in the almond milk, vanilla extract, eggs, and another bowl. *(4)* Combine the dry components with the liquid ones and mix well. *(5)* Mix in the chopped

zucchini. **(6)** For forty minutes, or until a toothpick inserted in the middle comes out clean, coat the loaf pan with the batter. **(7)** Let it cool completely before slicing.

238. GARLIC LEMON BROILED SHRIMP

Total Time: 15 minutes | Prep Time: 10 minutes

Ingredients:

- 1 pound large shrimp, peeled and deveined
- 2 tablespoons fresh lemon juice
- ½ teaspoon paprika
- ¼ teaspoon black pepper
- 1 tablespoon fresh parsley, chopped
- 2 tablespoons olive oil
- 2 garlic cloves, minced
- ½ teaspoon salt
- ¼ teaspoon red pepper flakes (optional)

Directions:

(1) Set a baking sheet on a preheated broiler pan. **(2)** Combine the olive oil, ground garlic, red pepper flakes, salt, lemon juice, paprika, and black pepper in a bowl and mix with a whisk. Incorporate the shrimp and mix to coat. **(3)** Place the shrimp in one layer per sheet pan. **(4)** The shrimp should be opaque and cooked through after 5 minutes of broiling, turning once halfway through. **(5)** Before serving, garnish with fresh parsley.

239. PESTO SHRIMP SALAD

Total Time: 15 minutes | Prep Time: 10 minutes | Cook Time: 5 minutes

Ingredients:

- 1 lb shrimp, peeled and deveined
- 2 tbsp olive oil
- ½ tsp sea salt
- 2 cups baby spinach
- ½ cup cucumber, diced
- ¼ cup fresh basil leaves
- 2 tbsp lemon juice
- ¼ tsp black pepper
- 1 cup cherry tomatoes, halved
- ¼ cup red onion, thinly sliced
- ¼ cup pesto sauce (store-bought or homemade)

Directions:

(1) Grease a pan and place it on a medium heat setting. Sauté the shrimp for three to four minutes on each side or until they become opaque and pink, adding salt and pepper as needed. **(2)** Put the basil, cherry tomatoes, cucumber, red onion, and spinach in a big bowl. **(3)** Add the lemon juice and pesto sauce to the heated shrimp and toss to combine. **(4)** Toss the salad with the shrimp, stir carefully, and serve right away.

240. HERB BUTTER ROASTED TURKEY

Total Time: 2 hours 30 minutes | Prep Time: 15 minutes | Cook Time: 2 hours 15 minutes

Ingredients:

- 1 small turkey (about 5 lbs)
- 1 tbsp olive oil
- 1 tsp black pepper
- 1 tbsp fresh rosemary, chopped
- 1 tbsp fresh parsley, chopped
- 4 garlic cloves, whole
- ¼ cup unsalted butter, softened
- 2 tsp sea salt
- 2 tsp garlic powder
- 1 tbsp fresh thyme, chopped
- 1 lemon, sliced
- 1 cup chicken broth

Directions:

(1) Get your oven preheated to 375°F, which is 190°C. **(2)** To dry the turkey, pat it with paper towels. **(3)** Combine olive oil, rosemary, parsley, garlic powder, salt, pepper, and butter in a small bowl. **(4)** Spread the herb butter evenly over the turkey, being sure to get beneath the skin as well. **(5)** Place sliced lemons and entire garlic cloves into the turkey's cavity. **(6)** Add the chicken stock to a roasting pan and add the turkey. **(7)** Roast at a temperature of 165°F (74°C) for two hours, basting halfway through. **(8)** Allow to cool for fifteen minutes before carving.

241. ROASTED CAULIFLOWER CURRY

Total Time: 35 minutes | Prep Time: 10 minutes | Cook Time: 25 minutes

Ingredients:

1 head cauliflower, cut into florets	2 tbsp olive oil
1 tsp sea salt	½ tsp black pepper
1 tsp turmeric	1 tsp ground cumin
1 tsp ground coriander	½ tsp paprika
1 can (14 oz) coconut milk	1 cup diced tomatoes
½ cup onion, chopped	2 garlic cloves, minced
1-inch piece ginger, grated	1 tbsp curry powder
½ tsp red pepper flakes (optional)	½ cup fresh cilantro, chopped

Directions:

(1) Set oven temperature to 400°F. **(2)** Combine one tablespoon of olive oil, salt, pepper, turmeric, cumin, and coriander with the cauliflower florets. Toss to coat. Bake for twenty minutes. **(3)** Put the remaining olive oil in a large saucepan and set it over medium heat. Put in the garlic, ginger, and onion and cook them until they're tender. **(4)** Add the coconut milk, chopped tomatoes, red pepper flakes, curry powder, and paprika. Stir to combine. Low heat for five minutes. **(5)** Coat the roasted cauliflower by adding it and stirring. Sauté for a further five minutes. **(6)** Warm the dish before serving, and top with chopped cilantro.

242. GRILLED HALLOUMI SALAD

Total Time: 20 minutes | Prep Time: 10 minutes | Cook Time: 10 minutes

Ingredients:

8 oz halloumi cheese, sliced	1 tbsp olive oil
4 cups mixed greens	1 cup cherry tomatoes, halved
½ cup cucumber, sliced	¼ cup red onion, thinly sliced
2 tbsp fresh mint leaves	2 tbsp lemon juice
2 tbsp balsamic glaze	1 tbsp toasted sesame seeds

Directions:

(1) Bring a grill pan to a medium heat. **(2)** Olive oil the halloumi slices and grill them for two or three minutes on each side or until they become golden brown. **(3)** Combine mixed greens, mint, cherry tomatoes, cucumber, and red onion in a large bowl. Top with grilled halloumi. **(4)** Add balsamic glaze and lemon juice. Before serving, top with sesame seeds.

243. LOW-CARB STUFFED CABBAGE ROLLS

Total Time: 1 hour 10 minutes | Prep Time: 20 minutes

Ingredients:

1 head green cabbage	1 lb ground turkey or lean beef
1 small onion, finely chopped	1 clove garlic, minced
1 cup cauliflower rice	1 egg
1 tsp dried oregano	1 tsp smoked paprika
½ tsp salt	¼ tsp black pepper
1 ½ cups sugar-free marinara sauce	½ cup shredded mozzarella cheese (optional)

Directions:

(1) Get the oven hot, about 375 degrees Fahrenheit. **(2)** Heat up a big saucepan of water until it boils. Blanch 10–12 big cabbage leaves for 2–3 minutes or until they are tender. Peel them carefully. Detach and put aside. **(3)** Throw the ground turkey, garlic, onion, cauliflower rice, egg, oregano, paprika, salt, and pepper into a big bowl. **(4)** Roll up the cabbage leaves firmly after stuffing each one with a tablespoon of filling. **(5)** Divide the marinara in half and spread it equally on the baking dish's bottom. Top the dish with the cabbage rolls, seam side down. **(6)** Distribute the leftover marinara sauce evenly among the buns. Bake for forty minutes with the foil on top. **(7)** Bake for a further 10 minutes or until cheese melts, if using. After that, uncover and top with mozzarella. **(8)** Keep heated before serving.

244. CRISPY BAKED TOFU NUGGETS

Total Time: 35 minutes | Prep Time: 10 minutes

Ingredients:

1 block (14 oz) extra-firm tofu, pressed and cubed	2 tbsp olive oil
½ cup almond flour	2 tbsp nutritional yeast
1 tsp smoked paprika	1 tsp garlic powder
½ tsp salt	½ tsp black pepper
1 egg, beaten	

Directions:

(1) Bring the oven up to a high temperature (400°F). Sprinkle parchment paper on a baking pan. **(2)** The almond flour, nutritional yeast, paprika, garlic powder, salt, and pepper should be combined in a shallow plate. **(3)** Coat the tofu cubes in the almond flour mixture after dipping them in the beaten egg. **(4)** Using a baking sheet, arrange the coated tofu nuggets. Put a little olive oil on top. **(5)** Cook, turning once halfway through, for 25 minutes or until crisp and golden. **(6)** Pair with a low-carb dipping sauce or sugar-free ketchup.

245. HERB BUTTER BAKED TROUT

Total Time: 25 minutes | Prep Time: 5 minutes

Ingredients:

2 trout fillets (about 6 oz each)	2 tbsp butter, softened
1 tbsp fresh parsley, chopped	1 tsp fresh dill, chopped
1 clove garlic, minced	½ tsp salt
¼ tsp black pepper	1 tbsp lemon juice
1 tsp olive oil	

Directions:

(1) Bring the oven up to a high temperature (400°F). Before lining a baking pan with foil, brush it with a small amount of olive oil. **(2)** Combine the butter, dill, parsley, garlic, salt, and pepper in a small bowl. **(3)** After that, lay the fillets of fish skin-side down on the baking pan. Make sure to coat each fillet equally with the herb butter. **(4)** Add a squeeze of lemon juice. **(5)** Flake the fish easily with a fork after 15 minutes in the oven. **(6)** Warm it up and serve it with some steamed veggies or a green salad.

246. ASIAN GRILLED CHICKEN SKEWERS

Total Time: 40 minutes (includes marinating time) | Prep Time: 10 minutes

Ingredients:

1 lb chicken breast, cut into cubes	2 tbsp coconut aminos
1 tbsp sesame oil	1 tbsp rice vinegar
1 clove garlic, minced	½ tsp ginger, grated
½ tsp red pepper flakes	1 tsp sesame seeds (optional)
1 red bell pepper, cut into chunks	1 zucchini, sliced
8 wooden skewers soaked in water	

Directions:

(1) Mix together the sesame oil, ginger, garlic, red pepper flakes, rice vinegar, coconut aminos, and rice in a bowl. After 20 minutes of marinating, add the cubes of chicken. **(2)** Heat up a grill pan or outside grill to medium heat. **(3)** Prepare skewers by threading zucchini, bell peppers, and chicken. **(4)** Grill the chicken for four to five minutes on each side or until it is fully cooked and has grill marks. **(5)** Add sesame seeds on top before serving. Snack on some cauliflower rice and savor.

247. SHRIMP ZOODLE SCAMPI

Total Time: 20 minutes | Prep Time: 10 minutes | Cook Time: 10 minutes

Ingredients:

1 lb shrimp, peeled and deveined	2 medium zucchini, spiralized into zoodles
2 tbsp olive oil	3 cloves garlic, minced
½ cup cherry tomatoes, halved	¼ tsp red pepper flakes (optional)
¼ cup low-sodium chicken broth	2 tbsp lemon juice
¼ cup grated Parmesan cheese (optional)	2 tbsp fresh parsley, chopped
Salt and black pepper to taste	

Directions:

(1) In a big skillet, heat up one tablespoon of olive oil over medium heat. Before adding the shrimp, make sure they are pink and opaque. Season with salt and black pepper. Cook for about 2 minutes on each side. After taking it out of the pan, put it aside. **(2)** Toss in the garlic and leftover olive oil in the same pan. Reduce heat and sauté for 30 seconds or until the aroma begins to waft. **(3)** Red pepper flakes and cherry tomatoes should be added now. To begin softening the tomatoes, cook for 2 minutes. **(4)** To deglaze the pan, pour in the chicken stock and lemon juice and swirl to combine. Two minutes is all it needs to simmer. **(5)** Incorporate the zucchini zoodles and mix well. Be careful not to overcook; you want it just delicate but not completely soft. **(6)** Put the shrimp back in the pan and toss them around again. **(7)** If desired, top with grated Parmesan and chopped fresh parsley just before serving.

248. SESAME CHICKEN CAULIFLOWER RICE

Total Time: 25 minutes | Prep Time: 10 minutes | Cook Time: 15 minutes

Ingredients:

2 boneless, skinless chicken breasts	2 tbsp avocado oil or sesame oil
3 tbsp low-sodium soy sauce	1 tbsp rice vinegar
1 tbsp sesame seeds	2 cloves garlic, minced
1 tsp grated ginger	1 tbsp honey or sugar-free sweetener
½ tsp red pepper flakes (optional)	3 cups cauliflower rice
½ cup green onions, chopped	½ cup bell peppers, diced
½ cup broccoli florets	Salt and black pepper to taste

Directions:

(1) Using a medium-high heat source, warm one tablespoon of avocado oil in a big pan. Toss in the chicken and sprinkle with some black pepper and salt. Turn after 5 or 6 minutes or until cooked through and golden brown. Detach and put aside. **(2)** Toss in the ginger and garlic with the leftover oil in the same skillet. Saute for a minute. **(3)** Bring the broccoli and bell peppers to a stir. Just short of tender, cook for three minutes. **(4)** After two or three minutes of stirring, add the rice made from cauliflower. **(5)** In a small bowl, stir together the red pepper flakes, rice vinegar, soy sauce, and honey. Stir the cauliflower rice mixture well before pouring it over. **(6)** After the chicken has cooked, add it back to the pan and mix everything well. Add two more minutes of cooking time. **(7)** Add some green onions and sesame seeds as a garnish before serving.

THE END

Printed in Great Britain
by Amazon

ecea30bf-4a1a-4289-b86c-134350bff079R01